Pain and Awakening

A personal experience of healing chronic pain, depression, and trauma using conscious awareness.

Brenda Nolan

Table of Contents

Introduction

The pain was unbearable, but it wasn't going to kill me. It was the illness that brought forward the precipice of death. I had been brow-beaten by doctors and therapists for decades. The dosage of medications and complications of disease cost my broken body the ability to digest food. This body had been vomiting any sustenance I tried to feed it. The ability to wash myself had been gone for months and I was barely able to leave my bed or behave as the wife and mother my family needed. As I lay alone in my bed that night, emaciated and exhausted, I knew it was the last time I would see my husband and children. Their years of constant caregiving would soon be over.

Death had been looming for weeks, and I was ready for the adventure. I waited for it like a grand graduation from my own personal hell. The pain was about to be over. The illness was about to win.

I still don't understand how I woke up.

Perhaps telling this story is the reason why.

There is a prominent saying that goes something like this, "One cannot learn how to swim from reading a book."

Yes, there are examples of people reading books then getting in water and swimming – but the same thing happens if you give a child simple instruction and then throw them in the deep end. They are likely going to survive. I don't recommend it, but it holds true.

If you're reading this, you've probably been thrown in the "deep end" of pain. Perhaps there is something in you that recognizes conscious awareness and is seeking out more knowledge.

I'd love to pour what I've learned about conscious awakening through pain into everyone's cup. I'd love to watch knowledge overflow in others with the sense of peace and serenity that I have found. It is not something I can do. As much as I have experienced in my life, the ability to convey this knowledge with complete understanding on the other end is not known to me.

The best I can do is write down my experiences and practices with the hopes that those seeking information and guidance can find it without drowning.

Pulling no punches, I'll tell you that the main ingredients to surviving pain is happiness and hope.

Happiness is more than just an emotion. It's the lifebuoy that keeps us afloat amidst a deluge of turmoil. Though you may experience emotion with external things and activities, that emotion originates inside your body. Happiness is produced from inside the body outward. Yes, external things can bring on the creation of serotonin, the body's 'happy' chemical. Friends, loved ones, exercise, substances, food, and alcohol can all help elevate our mood. Still, the ability to be happy and continuously return to this state resides within us all. I'm not saying someone can experience happiness from within all the time and never have any other emotion. I'm suggesting one can learn how to feel any emotion and return to happiness without external stimulus.

Learning how to return to happiness has been a key component in my journey with pain.

The next secret in my understanding is that I am not my body.

If someone cuts off my hand – do I exist a little less in this world? If someone exchanges part of my body from bone to metal, am I no longer completely me? Does the loss of an organ redefine my identity? Obviously, it will change how I live my life from that moment forward, but it does not make me a different person.

This body has lost a handful of organs, faced broken bones and medical implants, and continues to deal with disease.

The relationship between who I am and the body I inhabit has been a long and challenging bond. Born premature and healthy, with minor insignificant skeletal defects, this body grew into a cocoon of torment hanging off a tree of trauma.

For years, I could not escape myself.

However, pain was just a noticeable piece of this life. It was illness that brought me to the brink of death and beyond.

Now, seeing life through the eyes of an observer, I understand that the correlation between my essence and the parts of this body are not the same. Much like the universe, this body is a complex system teeming with life in the most unlikely of places. When this life stops, the body will transform into something else, and my consciousness will transcend into something other than this human form.

This is knowledge learned from personal experience. Twice in my life, I have teetered on the brink of death. The first time granted me a glimpse of another dimension. Similar to known stories of NDEs (near-death experiences), my consciousness was aware of colors, lights, and sensations beyond my comprehension.

The second experience came after a prolonged battle with illness. When my body was unable to continue fighting, I gave in to the illness. I was exhausted, defeated, and already knew not to fear death. When I stopped fighting, the decision to accept death brought peace to my soul. However, this body was not willing to submit as easily.

It should have been the end ... in a sense, it was.

What I awoke with the following day was the knowledge that cannot be poured into another cup. There are not enough words in any language to explain what took place. If I had to choose a way to convey the experience, it would be with music and art.

Despite losing consciousness to the disease that night, the breaking of the new day was miraculously brilliant. A new sense of clarity awakened within me. My understanding of self and existence underwent a profound metamorphosis.

I was able to understand that pain had been trying to communicate with me, for years. The unsuccessful surgeries and longstanding illness had not diminished this form's power. If anything, it proved the resilience of the body. I simply had not learned to decipher its language.

Understanding the language of pain was not the only awareness I woke up with. A new depth of consciousness melded into my thought procedure. Somehow, I was able to separate observable facts from ideas that were produced in my mind. There was a gap, a space in my new cognitive process, halting my habitual rush to judgment. I no longer witnessed things with an instant label of right or wrong - good or bad. Every new experience became a simple fact stripped of emotional bias.

Instead of immediately deciding I did not like something, I was processing information on a new level. There were situations I accepted rather than wanting to change. For example, (when I was strong enough to walk safely) trash scattered at the local park did not upset me. I picked it up and threw it away without thinking of how it came to be there or who was responsible.

A few years ago, I would have been disappointed. I may have complained to my companion or looked around to see who would have left such a mess. My mind would have instantly compared that person to someone who leaves their empty shopping cart in the middle of a grocery store parking lot. The same trash might have even been dropped by a park worker carelessly emptying the bins instead of doing their job correctly.

My new conscious awareness never thought of another person when it came to the scattered trash. My thoughts imagined the wind carrying light paper across a field. I would see myself picking up the trash thinking it was a great way to strengthen my walking skills. There was no longer any 'bad person' to randomly splatter with blame.

Another strange development was how I learned to interact with other people. I was not a fan of meeting new people or even talking to people I already knew. Prior to my conscious changes, I would have been as antisocial as one could tolerate. This was the best scenario as long as I was in a good mood. If anything rubbed me the wrong way or pushed my buttons, my mouth would have shot off a list of swear words a mile long. My behavior would have been negative for hours or even days.

Now, with just a small gap in my awareness, I was able to understand that my quick judgment had caused my attitude in almost every situation.

Somehow conversations turned into opportunities to listen without the filter of my trauma. New and formerly uncomfortable situations presented themselves to my awareness as a new potential for growth.

I am grateful for the gifts I received through surviving pain and illness. Still, I can't simply hand them over to anyone. All I can do is share my journey.

Minor changes in my life have led to excellent outcomes. New opportunities and adventures come to me every week, sometimes every day. All of it is because I follow simple daily rituals that once appeared meaningless.

Gratitude became my practice and happiness became my choice. It may sound ridiculous to attribute making my bed every morning to a higher appreciation of myself. Or how getting dressed every day improved my emotional state because I was ready for adventure. My inner work, acts of gratitude and small steps of discipline changed relationships with estranged relatives because I was no longer a victim. As silly as these changes may sound, these were the steps I took in my new life. This life, no longer amassed with suffering and desperation, is worth living to the fullest extent. Pain brought me to awakening.

This is my practice, and I am sharing my story. This is not advice.

I hope that by sharing my story, and a few tips and tricks, I can offer solace and hope for one person surviving with pain and trauma.

Chapter One

Pain: The Lifelong Experience

Chronic pain ...I get it. This sucks. You cannot have one week, one day, one hour, or even one second without acknowledging pain. Somehow, you become less human. It's hard to breathe sometimes. My pain took me to dark places. I didn't know then emotional pain would affect me physically. The realization of this connection is still dawning on me, like pieces of a puzzle slowly coming together in my mind.

What makes me believe I understand physical pain?

It's a bit of a life-long story.

One crisp morning, in the early 1980's, pristine fresh snow blanketed the ground. I was off to school, excited that I was getting to leave early due to a dentist appointment. Wearing my beautiful fuzzy blue coat, I noticed the other kids waiting at the bus stop. Without a care in the world, I started walking across the street for another day of third grade.

I don't remember the next events. In truth, I hardly remember anything of my childhood. What I will retell has been spoken to me by people who were there and the court case that followed.

None of us saw it coming. None of us ever dreamed it was possible.

A little hill in the road can make such a difference. While I was hurrying to the bus stop, a car appeared from over that little hill, just big enough to hide a small 7-year-old child. In the center of the suburban road, a car struck me head on, knocking me clean out of my shoes. Though the bus stop was marked and not new, the little hill was just enough to make my little body and fuzzy blue coat impossible to see.

I've been told the details of the accident many times. Parents, friends, and relatives discussed the events for years, wondering how I survived. For them, it was a difficult experience. For me, it was the birth of incredible fear and lifelong suffering.

The vehicle struck my right side, propelling this body upward and into a series of rapid disasters. The best guess was that the car was traveling between 25 and 35 mph. Vehicles were made very sturdy in the 80's and I didn't stand a chance in that battle.

Against the windshield, my right side was crushed like the glass. The force was enough to send me flying off the car and rolling through the air. I flew several feet before landing in the middle of the road. Again, the right side of my body collapsed on the cold concrete. Nearly every bone on my right side was cracked or broken. My left arm was broken, and my skull was cracked and swollen. This body, nothing more than a little seven-year-old child, went through blinding torment in a few seconds, due to a little hill in the road.

This is the beginning of my pain story. I've told this story the same way at least a hundred times. I let it come to define me.

In the end, the accident was decidedly no one's fault. The driver did not set out that day to hurt anyone. Nor do I think I planned on escaping school for that long. It was just how the events played out. I see this now.

Still, the cascading effect of the accident led my childhood events into lifelong issues. It also affected every member of my family. The burden of medical debt loomed over my parents. Our family was small and already falling apart. My healing from the accident was more than a little tricky on the family budget. After weeks of coma, multiple surgeries, and months in hospital our family fell apart.

I cannot imagine the toll those months took on my family. We were not in the safest home. My father liked to drink a lot and there were many arguments.

Shortly after being discharged from months of round-the-clock care, my parents separated. My leg was in a straight cast from hip to ankle, but I was out of that damn hospital bed! Still, there was no celebration. With the churning of old and dangerous family drama, we needed to move to a safer and more affordable location, and fast.

Halloween Fall of 1982

My mom, ever the fighter, carefully set up a bed for me in the back of a rental moving truck. It was a great idea! I could lie down the whole nine-hour drive from Wisconsin to Grandpa's farm in Michigan. My mom, my two brothers, and I high-tailed it to the Saginaw Bay area.

Well, we made it halfway before I needed to make a pit-stop. However, this was the winter following the car accident, and it was a cold one. Not to mention, there was no heat in the back of the truck. I don't remember being cold or mentioning the cold to my mother. I was just excited to go into a gas station. If you think about it, I really had not seen much public activity in a long time. I was in a hurry to get inside.

Stepping down into the biting winter cold, I heard a snap in the upper part of my cast. There was pain, but I couldn't possibly know that a single step would alter any plans for my newfound freedom. In that instant, my femur re-broke from the cold and sudden pressure. I didn't make it to my grandfather's farm that night. I ended up in another hospital with more dangerous challenges for my eight-year-old body.

Another surgery and another hospital stay awaited me, stretching out for several more months. I didn't know what the word traction meant. I only knew that I awoke from surgery with weights attached to the end of my bed and a pin through my knee.

I don't remember too much of the hospital stay. Memories are a bit tricky. To be honest, most of my memories are missing due to the skull fracture from the car accident. There were a few memories, like still-frames or pictures in my head.

I remember getting into trouble for trying to sleep on my left side. The nurses had warned me, but comfort was something I constantly sought out. So, night after night, I tried to turn on my side. Eventually, searching for comfort created a new problem. My actions had moved the pin in my leg too far to the right. It didn't happen overnight, but it changed the way my leg was healing. Eventually, something had to be done to correct the distortion the uncentered weights were causing on my femur and knee.

I know I was scared. I doubt there is an eight-year-old in existence that would not have been terrified. Everyone was wearing scrubs, the room lights had been turned up, the doctor spoke in whispers to the nurses, and my mother was holding back tears. They brushed orange-colored medicine around the holes through my leg. It felt cold. I couldn't understand why I had to stay awake. Every procedure up until that point had been done in surgery. I wanted to just wake up ...with everything all fixed.

The nicest nurse held my hand and blocked my vision as the doctor and two other nurses came in to hold me down. They needed to physically move my leg, adjusting the placement of the pin within the bone. This was a simple few seconds of excruciating agony, but it was my first experience with complete conscious awareness. My body's sensations were unnecessary and vague in comparison to the vivid reality around me.

I knew it hurt. I had been given a little medicine cup of Tylenol with codeine before the nurses came in the room. I felt them grab my legs and my waist to hold me still. Then, I remember screaming. The doctor held onto the pin in my leg and pulled the mechanism toward the center of my knee. I could feel my muscles and bone, which seemed to be crawling sideways beneath my skin. It was absolute torture... however, I didn't feel pain!

My throat felt tight with the scream that saturated the room. Still, I didn't feel pain! I was aware of everything around me - like I had never been aware of life before. Imagine having no physical sensation other than vision and understanding. Sure, I heard my own scream. Still, that scream made sense to me. The room was filled with people and monitors, and nothing went unnoticed. I could hear each individual reassuring me, even though I was making such an unnatural sound. I knew the nurses did not want me screaming. Somehow, I understood that they all had their own emotions about the moment and each of them were trying to do their best to reassure me. It was probably in the timespan of five to ten seconds before the adjustment was complete. Only then, when the nurses had let go and the doctor was leaving the room, that the pain came to me. When it came, it spared nothing. I felt physical horror completely once the trauma had come to pass.

That was the only time in my childhood when consciousness came to me. It was such an amazing event that I spent my life remembering and telling people that I had once experienced so much pain that my body refused to feel it.

It was summer when I was released from the second hospital. This time, I came out in style! I was in a full body cast. Imagine a solid contraption where your chest is wrapped in a pure white cocoon all the way to your knees, with a bar extended between your legs, and the rest of the cast compressed the right leg all the way down to the toe. Yes, there was a hole cut in the mid-section for all the personal business. My arms and left leg from the knee down were free to move, but crutches were not going to do me good. Plus, I was too little to maneuver in my wheelchair. Everything I needed had to be brought to me. Mobility was a distant dream.

It was only one super-hot summer, but without the ability to scratch anything. If you've never had a cast on a broken bone, I'll let you in on a little secret. As your body heals and the skin does not have a way to exfoliate the area begins to itch like a rash. That, and I smelled like a gym locker all the time, literally ...all the time.

It felt like forever inside that enormous cage. Within a couple of months, I had begun to grow out of it. The edges around my chest and underarms had begun to crack open. For a while, we almost thought they would let me out early! Instead, a set of x-rays had the doctor re-plastering the top portion of the cast to keep it stable. It seemed like there was no way out. Fortunately, all things come to pass, and I was released later that fall.

The following summer, after I had been able to start third grade for the second time, I broke the same femur again. This time, I was riding double on a bike with a friend when the bike toppled over. This was in the eighties. We would be lucky if we had single-person landlines. So, calling for help was not going to happen. I walked the block on a broken leg, supported by friends. You can probably guess; I ended up in a third leg cast.

I was hit by a car around the age of seven, and I did not get out of my final cast until I was ten and a half. By then, I had spent a significant portion of my childhood navigating the challenges of recovery.

I was walking unassisted by the time I was eleven. By age thirteen, I had healed so well that I became a cheerleader, seemingly unmarred by past struggles. The only thing we noticed was that I had a few issues with my right knee. Also, the leg had grown visibly longer than the left. When bones heal themselves after a break, especially with kids, the bone can overgrow in many cases. My right leg was an inch longer than the left by the time I was in my twenties.

It was also in my mid-twenties when a deer in the road convinced me to drive my car into a ditch headfirst, smashing my right knee into the dash. Then came the knee surgeries, just the little ones with the scope that gets the loose cartilage fragments out. I've had over a dozen of those procedures in twenty years. Thankfully, I was still up walking and working. Life was great!

Then, the arrival of my first child brought with it unforeseen challenges. I had a genetic predisposition to gestational diabetes (Mature Onset Diabetes in the Young) MODY, morphing into type-2 diabetes by the time my second child came into the world. I had adjusted to the disease enough to have a normal life. The only thing I had to do, in order to maintain a regular life ...was to not slip up.

Guess what I did? Thirty years after being hit by a car, in 2012, I slipped up ...literally. I slipped on a wet wooden walkway while carrying a fifty-pound box. I never fell to the ground. I contorted in several unusual ways on the walkway, twisting left to right as if dancing an involuntary and agonizing jig. Well, there went my back.

If you're reading a story like this, you know that feeling ... the one deep in your gut that says, "You seriously hurt something." Yes, that was screaming in my head. In that instant, I knew I was in trouble. There was no way I could have known that I had just altered the course of my family's future. One big box and one wet walkway ... that's it. That is all it took to turn my entire life upside down, again.

For over half a year, I was treated for three herniated discs. But I wasn't getting better. Instead of progress, I found myself trapped in a downward spiral of worsening symptoms. Pain invaded my lower back and pelvis. I could not stand, sit, walk, or lie down without facing a battleground of agony. When it came to riding in a car, I would have to hold myself up by the door's safety handle to avoid the impact of every bump on the road. My pelvis could not take any sudden shifts or movements. Life was becoming limited, difficult, and emotionally strenuous.

Finally, after months of complaining, my doctor pulled out a medical book and looked up SI Joint Dysfunction. The symptoms matched up perfectly. So, after an abrupt medical pivot, I was going to see specialists for sacroiliac joint dysfunction. The SI joints are butterfly-looking heaps of cartilage on both sides of the pelvic area that connect the pelvis to the spine. Since I was still dealing with lumbar damage, I had full body scans done at that time.

Oh, the surprises we found! My spine was a little more than crooked. The entire time I was busy growing up and hanging out with friends, my skeleton decided to take a left turn. The asymmetry in my legs had made my pelvis slowly creep up, causing one hip to be over an inch higher than the other. This skewed my spine in another direction. While the spine was twisting, those little butterfly joints (SI joint) were trying to fuse naturally by growing into solid bone. With each step, each twist, each turn, the process of fusion became an impossible and agonizing ordeal. It seemed like my actions were breaking down the natural fusion process.

For thirty years, while I was living a normal life, my spine was slowly rotating two separate ways. Suddenly, the illusion of normalcy shattered, replaced by a relentless onslaught of pain that would come to define my existence for the next two decades.

This led me down an endless odyssey of medical interventions including surgeries, injections, radio-frequency ablations (nerve burns), and drugs. Oh my, the drugs!

The story goes on to include a particular fusion in my lower lumbar spine. That surgery failed but somehow created more pain. So, we did the only thing left to try. I had a spinal cord stimulator implanted.

A spinal cord stimulator is a small mechanism with a long wire that holds about eight perfectly spaced electrodes. It is surgically inserted into your spinal column and gives off electrical impulses, like a TENS unit, directly in your spine. The nifty little battery pack is slipped under the skin, like a pacemaker, and voila ... little jolts of electricity run through your body. The purpose is to direct your mind to the sensation of the stimulator and away from the source of pain.

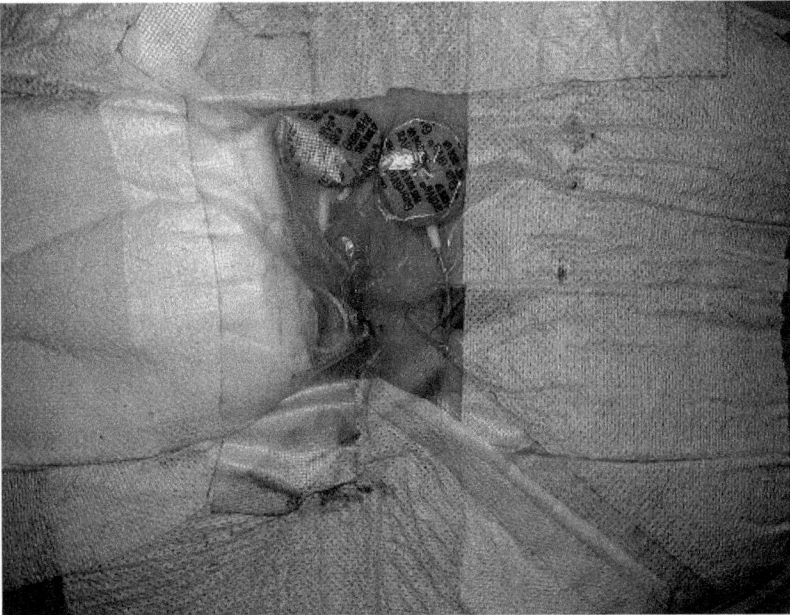

Initial spinal cord stimulator trial placement in lumbar spine

Though the technology was fairly new, there were many positive results. My research showed that it was successful in many cases. It was a great idea.

You do not know what decisions you will make until you are in a lot of pain. I was in pain, for years, and willing to do anything to get away from it. I missed walking, biking, riding in cars, and living a simple life.

Sure, I was scared, but it was so exciting the first day they turned the contraption on. There was a weird sensation, like a buzzing deep within the area it was programmed to target. (The placement procedure was done while I was awake enough to instruct the doctor where the sensations were being felt.) For me, it was hitting my tailbone area, and it felt strangely comforting. Whenever the pain increased, I could increase the voltage and the pain would subside. I was in heaven with how well it worked. I could finally walk unassisted. I could regain some independence!

That is, until 21 days later, when I was in the hospital, having the stimulator removed and dying of septic infection.

The next six months were hell. I had nurses coming to my home for weeks to assist with the I.V. medications and placement of a wound-vac. I was lucky to get the wound-vac. This is a machine that attaches to an infected wound and draws out the infection using a slight vacuum. It did not hurt as a singularity. What became bothersome was my allergy to every adhesive used in the medical profession. For months, this machine was attached to my back with, what seemed like, every kind of sticky substance known to man. Eventually, the itching became blisters. The blisters became sores. The sores became wounds. Finally, by the end of the affair, my entire back was raw with every inch of my skin affected. However, the spinal infection was healing faster than it would have been without the wound-vac.

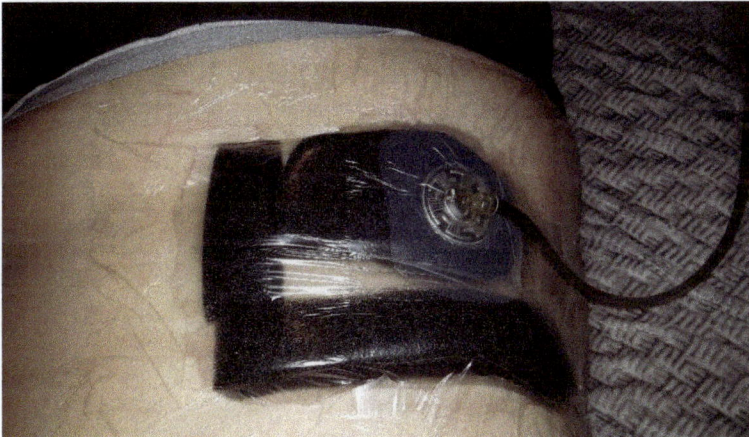

Wound-vac draining septic infection

It took a year to recover from sepsis. Still, the pain was relentless. Therefore, the only logical thing to do was have another device implanted. Right? I mean, what could go wrong the second time?

Well, apparently, quite a few things could go wrong. The machine was faulty. One year after the first implant, a malfunctioning electrical stimulating device was stuck in my spine.

The second spinal cord stimulator would not respond to my controlling device. I had no say in how often or how violently it would shock me. Worse yet, no one believed me because the electronic information did not relay the issue. It worked on a system a little like Bluetooth. A programmer would use an individual code to connect my device to their tablet and send instructions while receiving operational data.

malfunctioning spinal cord stimulator remote

The programmers who would see me and help reprogram my remote maintained that the device was not malfunctioning. I could not prove there was an issue. When my remote would show an error on the screen, there was no one around to show it to. Thankfully, we live in the cellphone age. So, a month later, when they would see me again, I brought pictures of the remote screen with error messages. At most, the team of doctors acknowledged that I might have a problem.

One night, in a deep sleep, I was shocked so hard that this body leaped off the bed in a horizontal position and landed smack on the floor in the same state. The jolt felt like shoving a fork into a toaster and being thrown across a room. Again, it felt like there was another injury and I was scared. However, by this time, I was gun-shy when it came to doctors. It took a lot to convince myself to get checked out. When I went into the emergency room to make sure I did not create more damage, after falling on the battery pack, the attending doctor asked me what happened, signed a form, gave me some Tylenol and sent me on my way.

It was on my way home that I read his release form stating that I was drug seeking and walked out of the hospital without assistance. This was a thorn in my side for days... since I already had pain medication and had already been wheelchair bound.

My trust in doctors was nearly finished with that visit.

It took eleven months to get the device removed. For nearly a year, I was shocked to the point of burning in my spinal column without any way to control or stop it. Months went by, until one new employee at the medical device company listened to what I had to say and looked at the evidence I had collected. It was because of her that I was able to get the device removed. I had gone through hell. Yet, I wasn't entirely done with my hospital fun.

By this time, my body was a wreck. I was confined to a wheelchair and needed quite a bit of help with daily tasks. In 2019, pelvic pain complicated the lumbar pain. Life had become intolerable with discomfort vastly increasing during menstruation. So, I underwent a hysterectomy. This caused some relief to my lower spine. I no longer needed to go into urgent care for a shot of steroids and pain medicine every 28-31 days. Still, there was more to be done.

Finally, in late 2019, I had my knee replaced. It had been on my checklist for quite a few years, and the opportunity came up that fall. Thankfully, that made a difference!

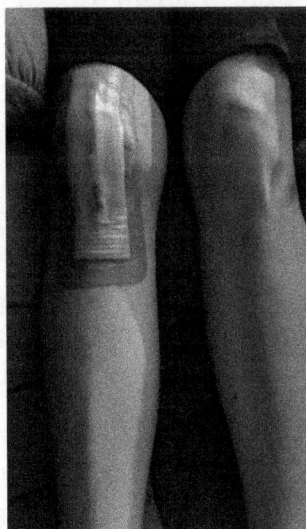

The knee replacement took a bit of the length difference away from my legs, and I felt a vast improvement. I was starting to walk. My back hurt, but it was less devastating.

This was fantastic timing since the opioid crisis had hit its peak. I had already been having a challenging time getting my regular pain medication. It didn't matter that I was enrolled in the pain clinic. I continued their rules and regulations, passing drug tests repeatedly.

Each refill had to be given in the doctor's office, a grueling 40-minute car ride away. This was mandatory. My urine had to be tested often to make sure there were no other illegal drugs in my system, and that the number of traceable opioids did not exceed the allotted prescription.

In order to keep prescription assistance with pain, I had to endure routine injections and nerve burns. Every year, and sometimes every six months, I would have to undergo Radio Frequency Ablations (RFA). This is a procedure where needles are imbedded into the nerve and radio waves heated up the pins to burn the nerve in hopes of eliminating pain. This would be done in approximately 12 to 20 different locations in my back at a time. This had to be done often, since the nerves grow back. Without undergoing these treatments, the drugs I had come to rely on would be withheld. This was required by my physician or insurance, depending on the time of year. The only thing I understood was that I felt as if I were ruled by a ringleader in a circus and the only way to move was within their circle.

Still, only two weeks after my knee replacement, I was denied opioid pain relief by my doctors. Not just for the knee surgery but for my spine pain, as well. This was a devastating blow.

I had been off opioids before. Every year, I took two weeks off to make sure I could manage the addiction withdrawal. Don't get me wrong, I admit addiction, but through dependency. Opioids gave me enough relief to walk unassisted. With a twisted spine affected by shocks, burns, a tilted pelvis, and failed fusion, walking was incredibly difficult and painful. Now, medication designed specifically to treat pain was no longer a possibility. So, I was forced to quit, cold turkey. The pain was incomparable, but I survived.

Then, there was 2020.

The medical world took a big shit during and after the Covid 19 pandemic. The doctors and staff were beyond exhausted and wanted nothing to do with my piddly little pain complaints. There was no way they would let me use hydrocodone after having been off it for a few months. There was a drug war being won somewhere, and pain management was seriously cutting back on prescriptions. Mine convinced me to try tiny doses of a new experimental drug. I had no problem accepting the challenge. The medication was something I had to gradually titrate into and play around with the dosage for months.

My body was slowly wearing down. My mental health took a nose-dive into depression. Pain was my constant companion. Situated in the regions of my lumbar area, bilateral sides of my spine, pelvis, legs and groin, there was nowhere to find relief. Even lying down flat would cause excessive pressure on my pelvis. My skin had begun to change color due to the amount of ice and heat I had been using to combat discomfort.

Within a year, I lost the ability to walk, again. A few months later, it was almost impossible to sit upright. At this time, medication for my severe depression was being increased regularly. I was led to believe that the depression medication would assist with my pain levels. Though my pain did not decrease, I cared a lot less about the physical sensations. Perhaps, this was my doctor's goal.

Then, came the illness. The experimental drug, which never treated my pain, along with a few other medications, stopped my body's ability to digest food. I was diagnosed with gastroparesis. A loose meaning of the term would be stomach paralysis. It can happen with the use of diabetes medication and the experimental drug I was taking for pain.

This is when things went downhill at a ninety-degree angle. Unable to walk, shower, move, or eat, I had hit my lowest point. The body had completely rejected the experimental drug and stopped my digestive system in its tracks. Vomiting and diarrhea became my new normal.

My nearly six-foot-tall body that was once a little overweight, just under 200 pounds, diminished to under 150 in a matter of weeks. This was the end of my faith in physicians. I was just done with it all.

For months, I stayed in bed, depending on my husband and teenage children for everything. My husband would shower me. My children would share small portions of their food with me. Friends and family were nowhere to be found. I know this is supposed to be about physical pain, but I had lost all contact with friends and family.

The feeling of abandonment was as critical as being hit by that car all those years ago.

I was incredibly sick and crippled by the end of 2020. It was not my intention or desire to survive any longer.

Nevertheless, here I am.

There you have it. These are the reasons I believe I understand pain. Truth be told, this was just a taste of my body's medical adventures.

I will never compare myself to another or assume I know the pain someone else suffers. The idea is ridiculous to me. There are many with worse experiences. There are many with better experiences. I am only here to convey the story of how I moved from my Pain to Awakening.

Chapter Two
What Pain Taught Me

Someone once said, "Life is pain." Very few life lessons come without pain. For starters... gravity alone trips you up and holds you down. Toddlers were given the term 'toddlers' for a reason. We learn to eat when our stomach hurts. We learn to walk when our knees are sore from crawling. Then, we are exposed to the complex lessons of life. All these achievements come with reward. Our pain passes and turns into new adventures. Which in turn brings new sources of pain. It's a cycle, but every step is worthy of pressing on.

I've learned a lot through my pain. It lies! Pain makes you believe you can't grow and reach your next achievement. I've thought about all of the lies I told myself when surviving pain. I felt I could not do the things I once managed. Pain sold me the idea that there would never be new adventures. There were times when I was tired of living. I thought the only way out was to make my own door.

I was wrong.

It took me a decade to learn that I had been selling myself short. I had been giving my discomfort more power than it actually held over me. The multitude of factors within my body created a prison. That prison taught me a lot about how to protect myself.

FIRST - ANYTHING UNFAMILIAR IS TERRIFYING.

When life was difficult and movement was unbearable, a simple invitation would send me into a whirlwind of fear.

"Would you like to go to a new restaurant?"

"Whoa there, Nelly!"

I can think of at least a dozen reasons, off the top of my head, why that is a bad idea. First, how is the car park situation? I can barely ride in a car and hate the idea of walking even more. How far from the parking lot is the door? I have to get out of the car, into the wheelchair, and make my way in between parked cars. We have a history of severe weather in Wisconsin. How narrow are the restaurant aisles? I don't like it when my chair is in the way of other people. Not to mention, if I get bumped, there will be an influx of pain. Oh, and how long will the meal take? If something happens and the service is slow, that's far too long to remain upright. My go-to position is reclined, and that is my comfort zone. Once I was invited to the restaurant, that comfort zone vanished! If we go

36

somewhere I haven't been before, it is terrifying.

These thoughts and questions took precedence over the joy that would come from any new experience. I learned to make excuses for almost anything I did not already defined as comfortable. I would exclude myself from social gatherings. I refused to go to my friends' homes because my wheelchair would be in the way. Anything unfamiliar was almost instantaneously declined. I wasn't sure of my safety! I limited myself before pain had the chance.

SECOND - PAIN MADE ME FEEL MORE IMPORTANT THAN OTHER PEOPLE.

Several times over the years, school presentations came up, and I would have to go. Funny, I never saw it as a treat or a gift. It was a challenge to meet. This is how I acted towards my children. I looked at their amazing accomplishments as my challenges.

I remember speeding into the high school with my wheels, barely on time. It didn't matter to me if people were standing in line. No one else was suffering from my pain. I was flying past people, choosing wherever I wanted to park my chair.

There was always an effort not to be in the way, but I made sure I had the best view I could manage, even if that meant sticking my wheelchair at the outside end of the aisle. Guess where? Right next to the exit. It didn't matter that all the moms and dads were there to support everyone. The moment my kids finished performing, I was rolling toward my escape.

My husband was not precious enough to be spared from my selfishness. It did not matter what kind of injury or discomfort he had to face. I convinced myself that his pain would dissipate in a matter of days, while mine was the true burden. This was my view toward everyone. Even those in my closest circle could not escape my selfish thinking and actions.

I'd be late for almost any appointment or event. It was impossible to drag myself anywhere on time. It was simply a matter of fact that the event would wait, I'd be late, or I wouldn't get to go. All three scenarios were simply fine with me. I could not be troubled with the time schedules of the world. My pain dictated when I could move.

My pain even seemed to breed jealousy. Somehow, my selfishness had become extensive. There would be charity shows on television or internet sites where families would receive help from the community or a particular series. Well, why not me? Those people had not gone through what I had experienced. They were being sent on vacation while their yard was remodeled, or their house was fixed up. What about my house and my yard? My pain fueled a sense of entitlement, convincing me that I deserved to be prioritized above everyone else.

It has taken years to see how wrong I was, and this lesson taught me to love others the way I wished to have been loved in that dark space.

THIRD - I STARTED TO RECONSIDER THE VALUE OF MY EFFORTS.

Pain drained the joy from every experience and extinguished any flicker of hope.

What was once fun became ...is this really worth it? Do I need to go to the zoo this year? Do my kids really need me to come to their parent-teacher conferences? My husband can go to his work functions with my daughter, right? I was in pain.

The weight of my pain made even the most mundane appointments feel like monumental tasks.

After a while, I couldn't be bothered to change my clothes more than once every two days. I wasn't doing anything in them, and everyone knew I wasn't going to tolerate being too warm or too cold!

The only joy that was instantaneous and never turned down was the ability to swim and be in water. Well, insurance didn't pay for the only therapy that actually took weight off of my pelvis and spine. My husband took me as often as he could. However, after a while, even swimming took too much effort. Getting up, getting dressed, and leaving the house just to return home in an hour... it became too much.

Then, there was all the piddly crap housework, cooking, and other tedious responsibilities. Everything seemed to be pushed onto my children. I was either in too much pain or, by that time, afraid that doing anything would cause more pain.

I stopped doing my hair unless I was going somewhere. The idea of cooking a family meal was absurd. The effort it took to cook anything was surpassed by the amount of mess I would have to clean up. The laundry was never going to be finished. So, I would accept that fate and not start the laundry ...EVER.

This became the biggest complaint of my family. Imagine not being able to bend or lift – now, think about taking heavy wet clothes from a washing machine and putting them into a dryer. Each article of clothing was over my weight limit once it was wet.

After a while, I wouldn't even get the mail. Oh, and it's not at the end of a driveway; it's attached to the wall outside my front door. It didn't matter. I was not going to open the door to get it. Pain made any effort not worthy of the prize.

FOUR - PAIN IS FERTILIZER FOR FEAR.

The simplest things began to scare me. Early on, these things made complete sense. I was afraid of going into large places alone. This wasn't unreasonable, considering I was relying on a wheelchair outside of my home. Grocery shopping, with its high shelves and cumbersome carts, posed a challenge. Don't forget the constant feeling of being in everyone's way. I was bound to be bumped, somehow. Worse yet, if my pain flared up suddenly, I would be stranded. Even though that wheelchair was incredibly freeing, it was also a significant cause of frustration.

I was afraid to take a shower without someone in the house. Our beautiful home was not ADA-accessible. Though there are stairs to the basement and second floor, I never ventured to use them. Every corner seemed fraught with danger, from wet bathroom floors to scattered toys that could send me tumbling at any moment.

Thankfully, we had devices in our home that could make phone calls in case I fell. I began to rely on these devices quite a bit. This gave me some comfort on my days alone. Still, I held onto my fear of being in the house by myself.

Family events became a cause of fear. No one lived near us, and visiting anyone meant a three-hour drive, one way. This was possibly the most painful thing to endure: long car rides. I was afraid of the pain that came with travel. Every bump hit my pelvis and jolted my spine. That fear entwined with my fear of recurring illness, and it became easier not to go anywhere. Also, I wasn't particularly good company. By that time, I was terrified of judgment and ridicule.

With the subject of fear, there was always winter. We live in Wisconsin. The average weather pattern from October to May is somewhere between "my bones are killing me", and "my joints are the size of balloons". I live in the land of, "It's too cold to snow." That saying is true and physically cruel.

Was there anything different I could have done? Probably. However, when fear has decades to creep up on you, it's hard to recognize how vehemently it can affect your life.

FIVE – DOCTORS ARE NOT MY FRIENDS.

My fear of doctors didn't develop overnight. It grew gradually, evolving with the fear of rolling eyes and heavy sighs. Describing pain is complaining. This can only happen so often before the complaints are brushed aside. It did not matter how honest I was or how hard I tried to prove my pain. No one else could feel it. All they could do was listen to me complain. Imagine the same song being sung on the radio for ten years. Eventually, it becomes background noise.

I was treated like a passenger in my health situation. I was patted on my head and sent away with a lollipop several times. My physician sent me to sports medicine. Sports medicine sent me to Neurology. Neurology sent me to Rheumatology, who in turn sent me back to Neurology. Eventually, my pelvic pain landed me in gynecology. Mind you, I had slipped discs in my back and neck, SI joint dysfunction, stenosis, and scoliosis ...and I was sent to gynecology.

One of my favorite memories was of my neurosurgeon after my spine fusion. He looked at the computer screen x-rays three times before telling me, "No, it can't be that bad ...this soon. Let's have you come back in three months and see if it improves."

I learned to have my husband speak on my behalf. He was a great communicator and

43

did not suffer the emotions that ruled my behavior. He was very patient at reminding the doctors of the roads we had already traveled a dozen times.

I was stamped with the label of a "pain patient," condemned to undergo routine procedures decided by doctors and insurance companies.

The worst doctor I had in my entire experience was my pain management doctor. Even after he placed and removed both spinal cord stimulators, he had no idea I was more than fifteen minutes of his busy day. The last time I saw him was just before routine yearly injections.

I asked him to be mindful of the SI joints. That was where my pain had been the worse, most recently.

His response was beyond harsh. His words were heard by everyone on the procedure floor. Even my husband grabbed onto my hands, fearful that I was going to strike the man.

"Your pain isn't coming from your SI joints!" He yelled at me like I was a bad dog. "Your pain is coming from up here!" At which time, he turned around and pointed at the lumbar region where I had the failed fusion, five years before.

I have not seen that doctor, or any other pain doctor, since that last procedure. It's hard to believe, but I must give the man credit. He made me realize there was no pain in the world worth being in a room with another pain doctor.

SIX - BEING A BURDEN IS PERCEPTION NOT REALITY.

My family had no choice but to take care of me. This also meant everyone around me had to live with the consequences of my imagination.

I imagined accidents happening over the tiniest details. Of course, I would have to explain precisely how trivial things could kill me. They could not possibly understand how the water bottles being pushed to the back of the refrigerator could cause me to bend too far forward, break my back and neck, and land me in the hospital! It was everything from the speed they drove around to the location of their backpacks after school.

I want to say my children did not resent me. I'd like to believe my irrational fears did not become a burden. Still, no matter what they were going through, my children had to care for their mother. On their worst days, their most complex, stressful, and heartbreaking days, they had to put aside their own needs to tend to mine.

I had no idea what was going on in anyone's personal life. There was nothing I could do to console my daughter when she needed a mom. Anything bothering my son was a complete mystery to me. Of course, there was my darling husband. He single-handedly bore the weight of our family for years, tirelessly caring for me as if I were royalty. Yet, he had also gone through three different job changes and his own physical trials but still fought to accommodate my needs.

With so much fear and limited physical ability guiding my everyday life, I knew I was a burden. This was inescapable. This body had become a useless mass of flesh stealing life from those around it.

That perspective nearly consumed me, but it wasn't the truth. Despite my physical limitations, I realized my husband still relied on me for emotional support at the end of each day, and my children sought my guidance and company. Though I couldn't always fend for myself, I found solace in knowing that I still held significance in their lives. It may not have been fair, and at times it felt absurd, but the truth remained: we needed each other in our own ways.

I was still there for the silly moments and the random conversations. I could still reassure someone that they chose the right outfit. I could remind someone to buy a corsage. Some day's my humor could help someone feel better.

No matter where you are on your journey, no matter what form or shape your body is in, you are not a burden. We are unique gifts of value and worth, simply by existing with those who love us! There is no burden when love is present. If the only thing we can do is love those that help us, that is more than enough. Believe it or not, they need love too.

SEVEN - DEPRESSION IS MORE DANGEROUS THAN PAIN.

I don't consider myself an authority on the subject of depression. My own battle with this debilitating illness has been long and difficult, and it was only through a newfound awareness that I was able to overcome it. For years, I struggled with crippling suicidal thoughts and a victim mentality. Seeking professional help was crucial in my journey toward healing. In fact, if it weren't for one particular mental health physician, I might not be here today writing these words.

If you are dealing with depression, I suggest seeking help anywhere and everywhere. I will discuss a matter I call "using the crutch later" in this book. If you have a broken leg, use

47

the crutch. If you have a fractured mental state – use a crutch! Do whatever you have to do to stay as well as you can. You are essential. The world needs you!

EIGHT– PAIN DEMANDS TO BE ACKNOWLEDGED.

(This was the most important lesson for me)

The uncomfortable degrees of pain are constantly changing. One morning I would be completely crippled. It would be hard to breathe. I couldn't even think straight. Yet, three days later, I could go to the grocery store and push a cart down every aisle. The severity changed often. Yet, I constantly felt like other people questioned the legitimacy of my physical restrictions.

Pain can rage like a monster. It can take the best of us and trample the light out of our lives from within. I've had several experiences with people just like me, those who have fought the battle too long and have a tough time holding their heads up. Many of them just needed their pain to be seen and believed.

I want to share two examples of my experience with others suffering pain that demanded to be heard.

I was sitting in the waiting room for my pain management appointment. A woman, nearing retirement age was wheeled into the office by her companion. This very patient man stood quietly as the lady yelled at him about the distance from the parking lot to the office. She was quite upset, and her patience had been tried and tested. Still, he was kind and courteous as the receptionist asked the aggravated lady routine questions about address and health insurance. Her answers were sharp and hurried, explaining that she had already checked in online. However, the man remained patient and sweet, rolling the nearly inconsolable woman into the waiting room to sit just across from me, a little to my left.

She was miserable. Her eyes were bloodshot, her legs were swollen, and she was irritably hot from the weather. She was visibly in pain. With that, she was not able to control her emotions. It was just before she started to cry that she kicked the footpads of her wheelchair and started fanning her face.

I took this moment to try something new. She was suffering and I knew what that felt like. I wheeled over to her and offered her one of the many hand-held folded fans that I kept in my purse. Women of a certain age don't like to be boiled from the inside out.

I had never approached another pain patient before. But at that moment, I knew what she needed. She needed to be heard. She needed to be seen and understood. Not for the person they were seeing in the waiting room, losing her patience, and getting loud. She needed to be seen as a strong woman exhausted from suffering. She needed to be heard like the silent screams we muffle at night, so we don't wake the house.

I offered her the fan and expressed my understanding of where she was in her life. An instant change fell over the woman. She saw me in my chair. She saw me with my fan, and she saw me in the same office waiting room. Maybe, just maybe, I could see the real her.

Instantly, she apologized for her actions. No one means to lose their shit in public, but it happens! It was happening to her! She tried so hard to apologize, and I couldn't help but hold her hand. She thanked me. I had barely said anything more than I understood. I had barely said more than ...three sentences to express it was okay for her to be upset. I saw myself in her. She needed someone to witness and believe her pain. Once that happened, when she admitted that she felt understood, she was able to calm herself down and continue a wonderful conversation. Most of the time, she complimented the calm, considerate man by her side. It was an easy situation to comprehend. Her pain begged to be acknowledged.

My Dad was sick. It was the only time I ever saw him cry. He had been in pain for years, and this was not the kind of sickness you heal from. Once, in the depths of his suffering, I witnessed his tears. It was a rare display of vulnerability from a soldier who had always been a pillar of strength.

I knew that cry. I knew that cry, and I went over to my dad with the same compassion I would have wanted at that moment. I acknowledged the warrior inside. Through a solid and crippling series of moments, I sat holding that soldier's hand. I watched him crossing his internal battlefield. It was only a few moments, but it felt like an hour. We sat quietly together. I told him I knew what it felt like to be held prisoner inside the body that is somehow betraying you. As his body shook, I expressed how sincerely I understood his pain and how he had no choice but to exist through those moments, alone. Dad agreed. Nobody could feel the pain for him. He had to endure the internal rage alone. We could only see the outside. We could not engage in his battle. A

man of few words does not acknowledge a
moment like that, but he squeezed the living
crap out of my hand that day, and he nodded his
head.

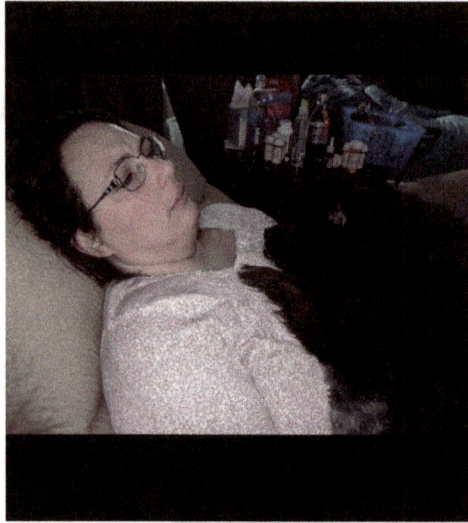

For those of you suffering battles that
your loved ones see but can never understand, I
see you. To those moms working the double
shift, barely able to function in your own body, I
see you. And to the men, standing so tall around
everyone when all you want to do is sit down
and quit trying, I see you.

You are in pain. Your pain is real. You are
a warrior unlike anyone could ever know.

Chapter Three
From Pain to Awakening

The years since have gone by in a blur. I'm nearing my 50th year. I'm walking everywhere I want to go and eating food every day as if it were never a problem. My illnesses are a side note, and my body is in check with what I need to do. I am happy and active. Heck, I'm currently in the process of learning nutrition and fasting to cure my type 2 diabetes. The best part is, I'm succeeding!

So, what changed?

I refer to it as an awakening. It may be a bit of a reach to say I'm spiritual, but effort is being made. There is no desire to become someone else. Religion is not my forte and there is no need to shave my head or wear a monk's robes. Although, they really do look comfortable. That being said, my awakening experience is with consciousness.

I am awake and aware that I have a choice in my thoughts and emotions. These are within my control. I am grateful to understand that my choice of action, in each moment, dictates the person I want to be.

Now, I do not have any idea why this type of awakening happened to me. Perhaps pain, illness and grief shook my foundation hard enough to crack. Part of me thought my mind snapped. I'm still not so sure this mind isn't simply malfunctioning. For this, I am most grateful.

NEAR DEATH EXPERIENCES

Before going into the experience that changed me forever, I'd like to explain the event that was the precursor to my current evolution. In all honesty, the near-death-experience (NDE) I had in my twenties was far more vivid than anything I experienced in my forties.

It may not be entirely relevant, but it was beautiful and partially the reason I was so eager to give up my fight for life. Allow me to digress to the previous event.

Northern winters can be rough. One particularly cold winter in Michigan, I was working as a nursing assistant in a home for behavioral and mentally challenged adults. As their caretaker I would come to the home they all shared, under constant assistance and supervision, and prepare meals, medications, and help with daily hygiene needs and other requirements. One shift, in the middle of a snowstorm, will stay with me forever.

The snow was treacherous and there was no going home. After a couple hours into my shift, after shoveling the sidewalk, I began to have trouble breathing. At the time, I was a smoker and thought it would pass. So, I struggled to breathe for the rest of my shift. Then, the weather turned worse. The nurses for the next shift could not make it to the house. This was not uncommon, and we were a close-knit crew. Of course, the lady working with me agreed, we would simply work another shift so the others could stay safely at home. Well, one shift turned into three. There was very little time to sleep, and my breathing had become quite labored. I thought I was simply getting a serious cold. Still, I finished the hours and went home when the roads were clear.

That is when things got interesting. Living with my parents at the time, I let my mom know that I was uncomfortable before I headed straight to bed. However, I couldn't sleep. My chest hurt from how hard it had been working to pull in and expel air. I noticed that lying down was beginning to make it worse and it was time to seek help.

My mom drove to the ER like a mad woman. Whew, I had no way of knowing how quickly things could go from bad to worse and I'm glad she was with me. Just as we entered the doors, it all became a shit-ton worse.

Breathing became something I didn't really want to do any more. It was incredibly painful, and I had been suffering for almost 24 hours. My skin began to tingle, and I couldn't even tell you how I ended up in a room on a gurney. What I can tell you is that when I was in real danger, there wasn't much fear. Everything seemed quite surreal. As my mom stood in front of me and nurses started hooking up all the required tubes and wires, I decided I needed a break.

It didn't seem like a big deal. I just needed a moment to stop fighting with my chest. How bad could it be to just ...take a break from breathing? So, I stopped. It was just for a moment!

Now, can I say I died – No! My pulse stopped and that is all I know. What I can say is, I had an experience at that moment. Perhaps it was caused by DMT being released by the brain. Perhaps it was a quick dream in response to my exhaustion. Perhaps there are a million reasons I can't fathom. Still, I know what I observed and that has been good enough for me.

When I closed my eyes, I finally felt alright. Nothing hurt anymore. There was no fear, no worry, no anxiety, nothing negative entered my mind. It felt amazing to stop pushing my body so hard. The experience was brilliant but gentle. The comfort was uplifting; however, it was only uplifting to a part of me that had been unrecognized before. There was a separation of some sort, but I couldn't understand it. It was as if my body were slipping ...somewhere else. My mind's eye saw light with intense spectrums of colors that cannot be painted with words. In that moment, I felt nothing of a corporeal being. I felt as if I had expanded within the light.

Around me, the room was buzzing with alarms and people shouting. My mom was crying and yelling at me to open my eyes. If only she could have seen what I was seeing she might have understood that opening my eyes would have been a severe downgrade to that current perspective.

I didn't know what was happening and I didn't care. It was such a fulfilling moment of grace, love, and unimaginable peace. Nothing hurt and I was safe. I would have stayed, if I could.

Now, other NDE's experiencers recall out of body awareness and voices of long-lost loved ones. Some people have said they've seen angels and ancestors they never met. Me, I saw only colors and felt painless and reassuring sensations. I have no memory of sound or voices, besides the distant buzz of the ER around me.

A slap caused my head to turn, and I started to come out of the vision before me. It was slow and I really did not want to follow the way the sensation was pulling me back into reality. Then, all of a sudden, 'CRACK'! My face was on fire. I knew the feeling of my mom's hand, and she meant business.

The number of tubes connected to my face and body seemed quite excessive. I had a nebulizer strapped to my mouth and nose and fluids were being pushed from two different IV bags and a huge shot had been stinging my arm. My chest was energized, like I had just been injected with jet-fuel. Finally, I kept hearing, "She's back," repeated between the people in the room.

Well, it's not an amazing NDE story, but it's mine. Again, I don't want to lie and say I experienced death. However, that experience did change the way I looked at death. I mean, no pain, brilliant colors, a feeling of love so profound it seemed to weave through my soul, and ultimate security... yeah, that absolutely changed the way I perceived death from then on.

So, when it came to the event that shifted my life's direction in my late forties, I wasn't scared at all.

Approximately, twenty years later, when disease and handicap brought me to the verge of death the second time, I knew not to feel fear.

Years of physical agony, mental strain, and months of starvation had broken me. Death and the memory of that realm of light and love had been calling to me with a voice much stronger than my desire for survival.

Day after day, week after week, I stayed in bed. Sleep was my escape. So, I started listening to sleep talkdowns and dream stories. At all hours of the day, I was trying desperately to put my body to sleep. Eventually, the stories in my headphones would end, and I would be listening to silence.

I hated silence. It left no room for distraction. On the worst days, when I could not find my phone in the blankets to change the video or recording, I would sit in silence, hating my body.

Eventually, as illness progressed, the times of silence began to grow. Long nights alone in my own bedroom became routine. I chose not to stay in the room with my husband. It would only keep him awake when pain or illness affected me. I was beginning to decline quickly. It wasn't long before I felt my body giving up. I really believed I was experiencing my last days. It was becoming very real to my family. Distant relatives were calling and even my mother drove two hours to come and see me. She left crying. We knew it was a dangerous situation.

One night I went to bed, knowing in my heart that I would never wake up again.

My spirit was broken from depression and pain. There was no hope. My family had suffered too much, and I was a constant burden to them in my mind. I was beyond physically weak. My breathing was barely noticeable, my heart rate had slowed to a snail's pace, and my skin was nearly transparent. I could not remember the last time my body allowed food intake. I was ready to die. It was inevitable, and I was looking forward to the relief.

However, that is not what happened. To be honest, nothing happened. Yet, at the same time, every single thing in the world vastly changed.

I woke up, surprised by the sunlight streaming into my bedroom. Its brilliance seemed intensified. Even the drab colors of my gray bedroom appeared more vibrant. This was at the tail end of winter, but somehow the world was warm and inviting. I can remember thinking that it was almost too bright.

My mind felt like a newly washed whiteboard. None of the old worries and concerns of life held my attention. My thoughts, empty of fear and sorrow, remained eerily silent. When I did have a thought, I stirred up ideas of gratitude and hope. Habitually, I had become used to waking up and dreading every day, but not that morning.

I had an emotion that was new to me. There was this strange feeling of accomplishment without having taken a test or creating some masterpiece. I felt happy.

Pain was within me, but it somehow shifted to the back of my awareness. Instead of rolling over and searching through the bottles and bottles of medications, I simply recognized that my body felt pain ...and I didn't need to fix it or dominate it in any way. It was no more apparent than the little white care tag inside my pajamas.

Not a single useless thought entered my head. I didn't feel depressed or hold any negativity in my mind. There was no dwelling on morning pain or lingering suffering.

There was one clear thought that filled my mind: I wanted ice cream!

It was about twenty-five feet from my bed to the refrigerator and cupboards. Uncharacteristically, my mind went into a focused mode that I had not experienced in a long time. I started to strategically plan my way to getting myself some ice cream. I had no doubt I could walk about twenty-five feet, but no further. So, that was the only thing I focused on. I got out of bed, made my way to the ice box, and got a dish of ice cream. There, I took a long break, bracing my week legs against the counter. Then, I went back to my bed with my dish of ice cream. I knew it was probably going to make me sick, but I didn't care. I did not fear being sick. I had vomited before, and it did not hurt for too long. On that particular day, I was content with anything that would happen. So, I ate my ice cream. It was amazing to taste but even sweeter because I did it myself.

My next thought happened to be, was I strong enough to shower? It was something I had not done alone for quite a few months, but I was feeling stronger after keeping the ice cream down for a few hours. As soon as I considered the idea, a realization dawned on me. The only time I was in real physical danger was when I was standing. So, the idea of fifty feet came into my head.

I had walked less than fifty feet to the refrigerator and back to bed. I could withstand another fifty feet. This time, the bathroom was only ten feet away. Once my body had fully rested from the adventure to the kitchen, I made my way into the bathroom. After a successful three-minute shower, I decided fifty feet was a pretty decent limit. Strangely, the only thing that occurred in my mind during that entire process was the exact motions my body was actively performing. There were no needless thoughts, no worries, no anticipation or expectation. I was fully aware of every detailed movement.

My first lesson, in living with pain instead of waiting to die from it, was fifty feet became a goal. Goals were a new concept. Still, I believed I could do this.

I can move fifty feet at a time!

This idea replayed itself over the next few days when I wanted to accomplish something. There were several naps, breaks, and sit-downs every couple of minutes. However, I could manage fifty feet to try and care for myself.

Strangely, within a brief time of adopting this goal, I watched a Ted Talk discussing the very idea. I had likely seen it before and forgotten. Still, this was a sign to me that I was on the right path.

The second lesson, if it wasn't crucial during those fifty feet, I did not need extra thought.

Like, when getting the ice cream, there was a chance it would make me sick. However, since I could not eat in the fifty feet it took to get the ice cream, I wasn't going to waste time thinking about being ill before eating. Fifty feet became my measurement of time and distance. This was what I had control over. It symbolized how much I could move and what thoughts could enter my head.

Normally, in any previous fifty-foot timespan my mind would jump from one negative thought to the next. I would think about depressing details. The floor was usually dirty. Cleaning anything caused me pain. Then, there might be depressing mail on the counter that would lead to financial fear. Any appointment on the calendar meant I had to deal with travel and criticizing people. Each of these thoughts lead to anxiety about who I had to deal with, what I had to clean, and how far I had let everything get out of control. However, I was only moving through fifty feet of space. That was all I needed to accomplish, in body and thought.

When I got the ice cream, I took each step with determination, and my mind stayed in that focused mode. Just stand up, walk, get the bowl, get the ice cream, serve the dish with a spoon, put the container back, and walk back to my bed. Each step was broken down into an action. Concentrating on those tiny steps kept unnecessary thoughts out of my head.

During the shower, it was a steady concentration of each step required to wash myself to the best of my ability. There was no need to focus on what I wanted to finish or do next. My sole purpose was only what I could do at that moment. By keeping my focus and intention where I needed them to be, I accomplished the once-impossible task.

This was my first step into consciousness. This was how I went ahead for the next week ...fifty feet at a time.

Then, when I did not have any function to perform, my mind held the same rule for my thoughts. It took me about two to three minutes to process fifty feet with my body, depending on the activity. Therefore, it became my intention to ignore any thought that wasn't needed in the immediate three-minute time limit.

How did I make plans? If someone is clearing their thoughts every three minutes and never thinking about the future, how does one make plans?

This worked itself out for me. All I had to do was be present and aware of what I was doing, at that moment. The point of this new hyper-awareness was not to limit my future; it was to experience every moment of the present. I still made plans. I was simply aware of every detail that went into making the plans. This meant knowing how the phone felt in my hand as I typed in information. It meant listening intently to what was necessary for the future, instead of creating imagined scenarios of how the plan should be.

Though I may be living in the moment, I am not oblivious to the future. The fifty feet and three-minute lessons taught me how to keep my focus on what I could affect. All thoughts of what I had to do next were saved for later. All thoughts on what I still had to accomplish from before were set aside ...for when it was time to do them.

Maintaining focus turned out to be more helpful than I would imagine. It seemed like I could complete tasks faster. Instead of starting the dishes and then stopping to fold laundry, I did the dishes with patience. I'm not sure multi-tasking is for me. I am unsuccessful at doing seven things at once. I find myself doing one thing and interrupting that job six times.

Living moment to moment was becoming a new way of life. I was taking care of myself more. Fewer days were spent lying down, and I was becoming better with patience and listening skills. Creating new goals seemed like an obvious next step. So, I created a lot of new goals. I wanted to observe and experience everything I could, without fear.

So, where am I now? Drug-free? Pain free? Depression and anger free? Not exactly, but yes, for the most part! I still have emotions. I still make mistakes, and my body still has hours where it does not want to move. The main difference is, I am better than I was yesterday and the day before that.

It took over a year to get off of fourteen different prescriptions. The side effects and physical acclimation were something I chose to tackle slowly. Everything was accomplished in a series of tiny goals. Out of everything this body disliked, it took getting off the anti-depressants the hardest. I spent about six months decreasing and stopping the use of each medication. I let my body shake. I acknowledged the muscle twitches. The mood swings came and went, and the shocking sensations that came with withdrawal occurred. However, I did not allow these events to compile into anything more than the moment they occurred.

There was no need to be afraid, I was learning how to listen to my body. If this body needed to break a pill in half for another week, that is what I did. It wasn't necessary to prove anything and suffer for no reason. I was allowing myself to heal from medications that I chose to feed my body. It took as long as it took and there was no pressure. I had a psychiatrist collaborating with me during this process.

All said and done, it took just under two years for the worst of the symptoms to subside. I believe the medications I took were completely necessary at that time. If it had not been for my awakening into consciousness, I would not have been able to let go of the pain and trauma that required medication.

For years after my extraordinary awakening into consciousness, I continued to set goals and push boundaries. The relationship I had with my body changed dramatically for the better. I had found peace. Additionally, I was constantly in a state of observance and learning.

WHAT DID PAIN TEACH ME ...SPECIFICALLY AFTER MY EXTRAORDINARY EXPERIENCE?

Conscious awareness is a powerful tool. It guides decisions and sways emotions. However, when one is dealing with pain and disease, the body can easily manipulate thought into unconscious fear and emotion. Pain wields such terrifying power.

It isn't just the pain. It's never just the pain! It is our emotional collection of everything that comes with it. I call this pain compilation.

Pain creates the idea of despair. It takes a rough moment and turns it into a horrible day, week, month, or even year. Pain lies. It makes itself out to be more important than reality. It dictates your emotions and promotes fear and despair.

I remember my pain. I remember how it had me beat down into a bed. Before I allowed myself to consciously experience pain, I did everything I could to avoid it. If my back and legs hurt, I would cancel all plans. There was no end to the creams, patches, ice packs, heat packs, and medications. I'd protect this body from anything that might increase discomfort.

It wasn't just for a while, either. I would cancel everything and wallow in my pain. This usually led to recurring thoughts of desolation, anger, jealousy, and guilt. This was pain compiling up into a mountain of frustration.

After gaining conscious awareness, I understood this body had been using pain to communicate with me. It wasn't slamming a prison door. It did not take all of my hopes and dreams and throw them away. Those ideas were created by the mind. Pain was communicating what actions my body needed.

Pain told me when I needed rest. Pain explained that some muscles and tendons required more or less use. Sometimes, I needed to stretch. Other times, I needed the help of medication to decrease swelling. Yes, one can go through life without using anything from a pharmacy. It was simply my choice to answer my body in the way I saw fit. After all, I was the one living in it. Just like you are the one living in your body. You get to make the decisions, no matter what a doctor or health professional dictates.

This body needed less movement with certain types of pain. I already knew this from experience. It was not routine. I could not say that every high-humid day would cause joint pain. Not every cleaning moment would land me in a bed for a week. Still, I used the information to allow myself more rest if needed.

This was also a product of awakening, knowing that it was my duty to care for this body. When it uses the language of pain to tell me to slow down, it is my job to slow down.

It might sound strange to address one's corporeal being as a body, instead of the usual terminology, my body. This was a gradual change for me.

I've spent this entire lifetime as this person. Now, with my current awareness, I understand that who I am is beyond the limits of this physical form. My thoughts are not the limit of my existence, either.

So, who do I think I am? In my deepest understanding, I am an observer of events with the ability to flow with life around me. Simply put, I am possibilities. Taking care of this body allows me to actively participate in the world around me.

As my curiosity for life and experiences continued, sound and vibration became an interest. At a renaissance fair, my son and I came across a set of windchimes that were over ten feet tall. The man selling metal yard decorations came over to tell us about the creations. He offered to push the black metal tubes that were too heavy for the gentle breeze. I stood there in front of the windchimes and felt the intense vibration of the huge sound. It was like being at a rock concert and standing in front of the speaker. I could feel the vibrations everywhere. I'm not sure if it did anything to improve my physical state, but I loved that experience.

"Mom, you look weird," my son whispered, as I closed my eyes and let the sound envelop the space around me. I love his honesty. I wish he could have experienced the moment with the same intensity I felt. However, his awareness was not where we were. It was not with what we were experiencing. He was thinking about other things and how he wanted to be somewhere other than where we were standing. There was so much to look at and so much to do, that he was uncomfortable with stillness. It is strange to think, many of us are uncomfortable with stillness.

As new experiences took me away from my bed, I found more chances to read and study. Also, I found more compassion for those on social media who needed kind words and empathetic conversations. By studying authors, neuroscientists, psychologists, and doctors, I gradually formed my conscious relationship with the human body. Then, I engaged in uplifting conversations with others in the same situation I had been in.

It may sound silly, but I consider myself a dense universe. From the moment of origin, this body has been expanding and developing. From the walls of my skin to the depths of my cells, every atom is alive. The fibers of my being have lives of their own, having formed communities and complex organs that work independently and in constant communication with each other. I am a multitude of factors that generate health, disease, growth, optimization and will inevitably decline.

My consciousness is my ability to understand the depths of this body and give attention to what it needs. In my opinion, my thoughts and emotions are tightly tied to the wellbeing of the individual organisms that make up this body.

It's great that I learned how to survive pain, but I do want to acknowledge that I also cope with disease.

The body is in a perpetual state of change. Sometimes, we lose weight or increase flexibility. Sometimes, we deal with sickness or broken bones. Then, sometimes we are diagnosed with disease.

Yes, our bodies heal themselves on a regular basis. We get a cut and within a week, the wound is healed. However, a disease is a little more serious.

A disease diagnosis is challenging to listen to and can be heartbreaking to think about. It means change is here. There is no more time to worry or plan. Life change is already here.

This gives us the right to be a little more selfish with our life. When our body is not acting like it did or how others do, the mind is bound to get caught up in fear and worry.

Please keep in mind, my way of experiencing life is not advice. With my diseases, I choose to acknowledge them as fuel for change. It is my job to assist this body, so it

73

can help me experience life. If this means I must learn a different way of living, I will learn and be diligent to these needs.

My challenge right now is helping my body gain the proper energy it needs in food that it can easily consume and digest. For anyone who knows me, this means I miss chocolate. I do. There is no doubt that chocolate is a rare and valuable treat. I also deal with digestive changes that make eating anything a miracle some days. On those days, I remain patient and spend a little more time reading and relaxing. Meditation is one of my favorite pastimes. I use these moments to remind myself of how far I have come on this journey and how much more I can do. I accept this body the way it is. There is no more fear.

I do not know how to implant a lack of fear into anyone's head. All I can do is tell you that the present moment is all there is. I cannot change the past. I cannot change the future. I can experience this moment. I can express gratitude, and I can change my thoughts. I will not plant fear when I want to reap hope.

Be good to yourself. Rest and meditate a little more. Judge the physical sensations as kindly as you can. Think of pain and illness as your body's language. Find gratitude for the work your body is still doing. You are a fantastic being with strength and wisdom.

We can still experience life after a diagnosis. However fast or slow the progression, the body is experiencing unusual sensations. It can be frightening at times and can lead to cascading thoughts of impending decline and unending suffering.

Try to be as calm as you can during the intense storms. Calmness holds great power by staying detached from judgment and fear. Let the diagnosis be what it is. We are still here, and we are valuable.

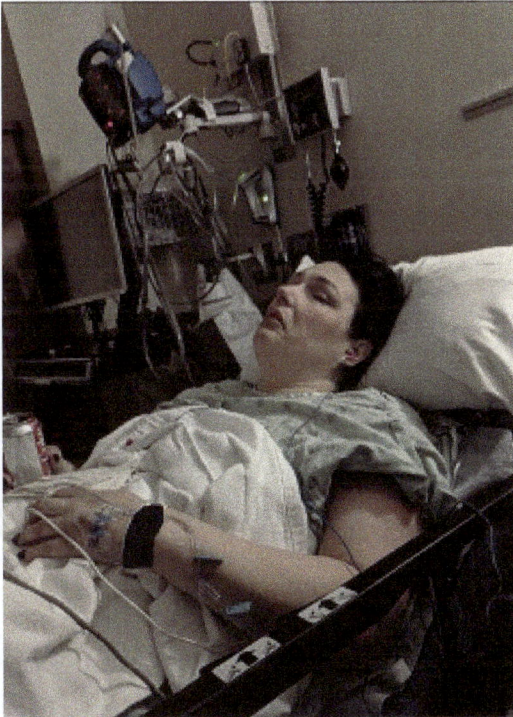

Chapter Four
The Sadness of Awakening

(Emotional turmoil and one big pity party)

By this point in the book, one might think that the expansion of my awareness was beautiful and lifted me from the shadows into the light. Wouldn't that have been great? To ...wake up with a new perspective and live happily ever after. Well, let me explain a few things about my shadows.

After my miraculous experience, as my thought processes began to slow down, I started to understand things about my personal history. For all of the doctors that I once blamed and all of the events I came to despise, one common factor was illuminated.

I chose all of this for myself.

Each test, every procedure, and the implanted devices had been my own choice. I wasn't a victim of life or luck. I was making choices due to fear and habit.

Emotional trauma surfaced like a stag with antlers sharpened into daggers, piercing through my psyche. If I hadn't hated myself before, I was definitely going to experience it in the months following my awakening. It hurt to realize my only enemy was myself.

The dozen knee surgeries I experienced, well …I asked for each one! Instead of changing my daily routines and adjusting my lifestyle, I chose arthroscopic surgery every two years. That seemed completely sane prior to my conscious awareness.

The hardest thing to admit was I asked for that damned second spinal cord stimulator. Instead of listening to my body rage against the machine, I asked for another! However, at that time, it all made perfect sense. I did not see another option because my faith was in science and the medical field.

In the weeks following my experience, I began to understand the ways I had grown into a fearful person. I could observe my past anxiety. I was always terrified of living in discomfort with a lack of security. Yet, that is what I made of my life.

Please understand this is not my opinion of anyone else dealing with pain. I will always recognize pain and respect the warrior living with it. This is merely how I came to know myself.

The limits of my body became a place to hide. It was easier to feel physical pain than to deal with my emotional issues. I didn't feel like I needed to talk to a therapist. I certainly didn't feel like my history led me to choose pain over unfamiliar growth. However, once my awareness sharpened, I could see my life was being steered by one hand on pain and one hand on emotional trauma.

My life is no more complicated than anyone else's. However, allow me to share a few highlights that led this terrified human down a path that incessantly chose pain and suffering over change and growth.

The predominant pieces of my past.

I'm going to lay out my memories to explain my trauma. At the same time, I'd like to explain how the memory affected my life and what I learned about myself through the experience. Of course, this is after my new awareness took place. As Oscar Wild once stated, "Life gives you the test first and the lesson second." Damn, he knew what he was talking about.

Alright, we're going back to the 1980's. I've already explained my early car accident. What has not been mentioned are the other events of that decade.

The early years of life are kind of a mystery for me. By the time 1984 rolled around, my family consisted of my mom, one older brother, and myself. Alcoholism played a large part in the separation of my family. The divorce of my parents took a few years to finalize. My eldest brother, nearly ten years older than me, chose to live with friends.

This separation was likely traumatic for me. I'm not going to lie, memory loss from the car accident leaves a lot of blanks in my history. This is one aspect of my life that I consider a huge advantage.

I'm sure on some subconscious level I have emotions left over from this, but I've never dwelled on what I cannot remember. There were horror stories that were passed on to me. However, with my current understanding of people and their perspectives, I have more questions than answers. What was real and what was fabricated?

THE MOST PAINFUL LESSON CAME TOO SOON.

Mom always said, "Love grows big in small houses." Well, we tested that out regularly. We moved around quite often. I do not remember all of the reasons we moved, and I didn't write the reasons in any of my journals. It wasn't easy picking up and starting over all the time. In fact, I hated it. I absolutely hated it. I never had a physical home. However, I was lucky! I never faced the first day of a new school alone. My brother, two years older, was my best friend.

I'll be completely honest, it was a love/hate kind of thing, but we were very close. We fought like tooth and nail, but it was never seriously malicious. I loved to tattle on him for any reason I could find. In turn, he would play pranks on me or settle the score another way. One of his favorite games was stealing my crutches. Sometimes, I would get up and hop around the house after him, but that always made Mom mad.

He was always with me. Every time we entered a new school, yearly and sometimes more often than that, he walked me through the doors and to my classroom. He was the class clown and often in the principal's office. One time, he even broke a kid's arm on the school bus, by accident. He wanted to show a karate-move he had seen. The kid with the broken arm volunteered for the experiment. Looking back on it now, I recognize that we really put our mom through hell.

She was, and is, an amazing woman. Mom was always working. She was one of those prize fighters that just never stopped swinging back. This meant my brother and I had a lot of time together. Like any pre-teens, we were stupid and found trouble more often than not. Still, he took the rap for me when he could and never stayed mad for long. Most of the time, he simply took care of Mom and me. He was our hero.

I remember one bitterly cold winter night when my brother was waiting by the window for Mom to come home from work. The snow had piled up and it was getting pretty late. He didn't have gloves or a snow shovel. However, that wasn't going to stop my brother.

Pulling two pairs of socks over his hands (double insulated home-made gloves) he went outside to the shed. He was worried the car would not make it into the driveway. Pulling out an old dirt shovel, he started to clear away what he could. I remember seeing two small paths, the width of tires, going from the house down to the road. He was cold and drenched from the wet-packing snow, but he didn't quit until the job was done. Mom made it into the driveway without any trouble. My brother was about twelve years old at the time. That little boy was the man of the house, and he took his station seriously.

It wasn't long before he became old enough to wash dishes at the restaurant where Mom worked. This meant that I got to tag along sometimes if I couldn't stay with a friend for the night. I was well protected after being hit by a car. If the two of them were going to work, I was going to stay with a friend or go to work with them.

This little rustic tavern became the new family we needed. The owners, bartenders, cooks, and even the polka-band became Mom's new friends. These people gave us a new start in life.

It wasn't long before Mom became the apple in someone else's eye. One man in particular had been asking her out for months. She was skeptical and turned him down several times. Thankfully, he was not the kind of man to give up on hope. Eventually, she agreed to the date.

It seemed like Mom couldn't catch a break. Wouldn't you know it, the night she was supposed to go out on her first date, her car broke down. Mom never did anything for herself, but at the first opportunity to have a night out with another adult, her car wouldn't start. Not only that, but the phone wasn't working, and it was downpouring rain. Their plan was to meet at the tavern where they both worked, but she couldn't even call to cancel.

My brother was not going to let our mom miss her date. It was just another of his heroic actions. He zipped up his coat, hopped on a ten-speed bike and rode nearly two miles to the tavern, through torrential rain. A little while later, Mom's date pulled into the driveway, led by my sopping wet brother.

Eventually, that new man became our dad! My brother made it seem like we had all won the lottery. Mom was finally safe and happy. We were all finally safe and happy.

Still, the two of us found ways to get into trouble, like digging an underground fort in the back yard and burying my brand-new pink glasses inside. He would teach me how to skateboard, and I would spy on his cute friends.

My big brother died in the summer of 1987. A skateboarding accident took his life quickly. It happened a few months after our mother remarried.

He had just turned fifteen years old.

THIS LESSON, THAT DEATH HAPPENS ...SUCKED.

His death felt surreal. I had endured years of hospitalizations and surgeries without any thought of death. It wasn't anything that I had ever considered. I don't think I even understood death as a possibility at the age of twelve. There had been months of uncertainty with my health adventures, but never the thought of death. It hit home too hard, too fast.

I now recognize this time in my life as my first really intense challenge. I'd get hit by a car a thousand times over if it would erase my brother's death. Nothing in my history was as painful as the demise of our hero. To this day, I barely comprehend the damage this loss sewed into my soul.

How could I trust anyone with the full knowledge that they could disappear eternally in a few hours? There was no goodbye. There was no illness. There was no warning. There wasn't a car to blame. He simply went to the corner market and never came home.

Sure, my father had left, my eldest brother had left, but they could both come back at any time. This was something completely new. This was death. My hero woke up one bright and sunny day and died that night.

Courage was no longer a strength I possessed after this lesson. My brother made me believe I could do anything. All of a sudden, he was gone, and I felt unsafe everywhere.

Consciousness did not change how much this event shaped my life. However, I have an appreciation for death that I did not have before. I recognize that it is necessary. I've held the hands of both my father's during their last breath and I've been at the bedside of patients who succumbed to their illnesses. As for myself, I have suffered within this body enough to understand the desire for fate. Death is a kind release at the end of the body's ability.

THE CRASH COURSE IN ENDURANCE.

Surviving my brother's death was hard. Surviving my mother's grief was heartbreaking. Even though I was there every day, even though I heard her cries and watched her struggle, I could never grasp the infinite depth of her torment. It was as if I stood on the bank of a river, unable to swim, and she was right in front of me ...drowning.

There was nothing I could do to make her smile. There was no place we could go where the lack of my brother's life didn't steal the sunshine. I had become the 'leftover kid.' No one ever made me feel that way. It was my point of view.

My mom faced incredible horrors in her first marriage. She fought to stand on her own as a single mother. She even worked three jobs simultaneously for a while. I remember she would have to cover her hands with Vaseline and socks every night in order to heal her blisters. When her son passed away (her heroic child) her strength transformed into extreme protection over me. Not only did she become protective, but she also became distant. I felt very alone.

We started to move again. It didn't matter where we went or what state we lived in. I was on lockdown. There were no more sleepovers with friends or relatives, and my physical health was a serious priority. I completely understood my mother's fear. Not to mention, I didn't want to leave her side. However, as time passed, her fear morphed into a severe distrust of anyone.

This inability to trust was a trait I willingly adopted. There I was at twelve years old, terrified of life with no trust in anyone.

I believe this is where I learned to withdraw from forming serious attachments. Maybe I formed this idea it from the nurses and doctors that came and left my life in hospitals, or the friends and relatives that would fade in and out ...depending on where we lived. All I know for sure is, I craved stability without permanence. I wanted the option to jump ship if life became difficult.

By the age of fifteen, I feared death, trusted no one, and my courage had been depleted to zero.

Navigating life as a young adult was a
little like a game of pinball. I moved around
between friends as the mid-nineties rolled on. It
felt like I was trying to find security with
someone. Hell, I even managed to get married
and divorced in the same year.

By the end of the decade, another car
accident forced me out of my nursing assistant
job and gave me a real chance at college. Well, I
didn't make it to graduation, that time.
However, I did get something better than a
degree. I got the news that I was going to be a
mom ...a single mom.

I wasn't completely alone. My parents and
I were still close, and my oldest brother had
come back into our lives. After becoming a
father and husband, he developed a great
appreciation for family. It was nice to hang
around his humor and creativity, again. So, this
single woman, pregnant, with a labrador puppy
and a blue '91 Buick Century, headed back
across the Wisconsin state line to my eldest
brother's home for a new start.

The pregnancy and birth of my daughter
was quite possibly the most complex challenge
of my life. By the time I was seven months
pregnant, we were both sick with undiagnosed

gestational diabetes. I had to be hospitalized in another state. Twin Cities, Minnesota was the nearest hospital with a fourth-level neonatal intensive care unit.

My daughter was born two months early. Despite routine care and tests, gestational diabetes had never been diagnosed. It was not a favorable mistake. For the second half of my pregnancy, my baby girl's body's teeny-tiny organs had been forced to process adult glucose levels. She was small, fed from a tube down her nose, and fighting for her life.

In order to provide the sugar levels in her bloodstream that would keep her system from crashing, the doctors had to feed her little veins a glucose serum. The process decreased over time, letting her system adjust as gently as it could. Though every safe measure was taken, my baby's veins could not handle the amount of serum. Needles and tubes had damaged both tiny wrists and ankles. Eventually, they needed to use the site of her umbilical cord to medicate the massive volumes of sugar I had spent months force-feeding her.

My tiny premature baby girl lived in an incubator suffering from jaundice, diabetes, and separation. She had never spent a moment in my arms since birth. The only human touch she experienced, besides my hand, was needles, tubes, and bandages. I could not even stay with her. There was no place for me in the hospital. I had no finances or friends to help with a hotel. I can only imagine my daughter's first emotion in life was abandonment. I forgive myself for this event quite often.

My first emotion as a mother felt like hell. I was alone. My family was too far away to make it to the impromptu birth. Everything happened so quickly. She was taken from me immediately by the crew of people standing behind the headboard of my bed. They brought me forms and papers to sign as they rushed her out the door and into a sterilized room next to mine. I couldn't see her, and I was still at the end of the labor process. My heart, my reason for living, and my entire surplus of motherly joy had been ripped out of my body and stolen from me. There was so much I didn't understand.

My health improved long before hers. I had to leave her in the NICU of another state for far too many weeks before she was healthy enough to be admitted to the hospital near my home. Finally, when she was nearly two months old, she was transferred back to Wisconsin. The hospital near me had a policy that mothers and babies would not be separated. I was given a private room with my daughter's incubator right next to my bed. Finally, after weeks of torment, I was able to stay with my baby girl.

This had been an incredibly weak point in life. However, I was no longer alone. I had my parents, eldest brother, his family, and a magnificent tiny human who looked at me as if I were amazing. I was not going to let anyone down. I am the daughter of a survivor who knew how to keep fighting!

In less than two years, I had my beautiful baby girl, a great paying job, met the man of my dreams, bought my own home, and held the ability to stand on my own. Oh, and I still had that blue '91 Buick Century (I loved that car).

As I dissected the events of my child's birth after conscious awakening, I was disgusted by my actions. I recognize that nothing could have been different, because it is done. Still, I chose to feed myself fast food and cheap sugar instead of caring for the body we shared.

I am aware that my incompetence was so thick, I put my daughter's life in danger. In fact, when my son was born a few years later, I still didn't know how to navigate diabetes and pregnancy. He was born in another state at a prestigious fourth-level neonatal intensive care unit, due to similar complications.

All I had to do was control myself. It should have been a firm choice to create the best environment to grow a child, but I was selfish and weak minded when it came to food. Recognizing this truth hurt. I did not give my children what they deserved.

THEY SEE ME NOW.

They see my determination to reverse T2 diabetes. They see me changing my habits and creating a better future. They see me fighting to stay active. Over the past years, they have watched me become someone new.

Back in the present moment.

Thank you for staying with me through the telling of these events. These pieces of history serve as a purpose for my story of growth and change. These memories, and a truck load of other dark moments, are the concrete and rebar of my personal pain.

When my miracle occurred, when I awakened to this state of consciousness, I became uncomfortably aware of how deep my emotional scars ran. Each of them needed serious introspection. Every single quirk, judgment, and personality trait required dissection at different times of the awakening journey. I wish I could say it all happened in the blink of an eye. It didn't. These changes in realization happened slowly over a period of months and years. I can honestly say that after five years of recovery I'm still identifying things in my personality that have a landmark in my memory.

It's as if someone has shined a spotlight on every foolish decision I have ever made. I am forced to view precisely how there had never been anyone else to blame for my past but myself. There was no bad luck. I had not been punished by an angry sky-daddy. In almost every situation, I took an action that caused the result I experienced.

This knowledge is uncomfortable and persistent. Thankfully, now I know how to respect these emotions. This is the discomfort of healing, not a new injury.

Some people call this period the dark night of the soul. Others might consider this integrating one's shadow self. I'm certain there are other terms for this. I simply considered it my personal hell. This person, my character, played the key role in all of my suffering.

Conscious awakening was not going to let me be aware of the present moment without forcing me to acknowledge the actions of the past. I was going to be a new person or at least a new personality. This meant I had to understand the one that needed vigilance and change.

My past was created by my choices. I had no one else to blame.

What did I fall back on to feel better about myself (without drinking) before experiencing steady consciousness? You can probably guess. I learned to hide inside physical pain!

The only time I felt compassion was when something was physically wrong with me. I was given the attention of a fighter during healing situations. Those who knew what I had been through would remind me how strong I had always been. Now, I can admit that the support system I craved was only there when something was physically wrong. Pain had become a place where I could hide from the world and recover my strength.

This did not mean that I faked my pain. My stupidity was far superior to my imagination. For example, one time, I wore a high-heeled pair of shoes to school and fell down a flight of marble stairs. When roller skating was cool, I smacked my knee into a concrete wall. Honorable mentions of injuries include yardwork, hauling holiday boxes, moving furniture, and letting a dog capsize my mobility scooter in the middle of an urban intersection. The ways I injured myself never ceased to amaze me.

Believe me, I never tried to create these injuries, either. I had no desire to face another leg cast! However, when an injury happened, people were supportive again. I mattered for a little while. I got to take a break from fighting life and stressing over challenges.

CONSCIOUSNESS DOES NOT COME WITH A SYMPATHY MODE.

Every memory I used to feel sorry for myself became a slap in my face. For each person I hated and blamed, I felt a similar way about myself. The person I loathed the most was the one I was changing. For the first time, with the help of my new awareness, I recognized myself as the puppet and the puppet master.

I want to say that I took this information and dealt with it like a sensible adult. Nope! I crammed every detail of my new realizations down my family's throat. I insisted that I now had all the answers to my life questions. Again, my immediate family had to deal with more "crazy mom" issues.

Remember how I pointed out that I was existing fifty feet and three minutes at a time? This was true! However, the emotional deep dives were occasions when my mind would force me to examine my habits and behaviors. Much of this was caused and healed through meditation.

This new conscious awareness was figuring out how to change the patterns that would not serve my future. I would take a situation on television or online and recall personal events, with good reason. I had been challenging my body, while my new awareness was challenging my soul. There was internal healing to be done, and I did not have a choice but to view my life from this new perspective.

It took months, if not years, to acclimate to my new awareness. Still, each emotional issue that was dealt with meant that I could make new and wiser decisions in my present moment.

The most significant part of my healing was emotional. My choices demanded to be acknowledged and investigated. Everything new was compared to old choices and their consequences. I had to learn how to let go of resentment. I had to dive into my past and learn how to forgive myself.

The key takeaway here is: acknowledge, let go, and forgive. I was not able to love who I was becoming until I learned how to forgive myself for who I was in the past.

This inner work is creating a better person. All of my old fears have been transformed into hope. Many emotional scars have been eradicated. I no longer dwell on past ideation. Nor do I blame others for where I am in this life.

Would you believe this transformation helps me live a better life with my physical disabilities? I'm not exhausted anymore. I'm not hiding within the pain. I'm not worried about hurting myself anymore. There are a million new risks I am willing to take, without fear. I am worthy of new adventures and new experiences! This life may have had a difficult start, but I've got the hang of it now.

When the pain comes, I rest. When emotions arise, I dissect them carefully without judgment. When opportunities come ... I will be ready.

I hold the key to healing my unseen suffering. With this key, I acknowledge the pain, let go of the guilt, and forgive myself.

Chapter Five

Conscious Steps to creating a better life

Although consciousness cannot be poured into a cup, it can be learned. Likewise, there is no way I can change my pain or anyone else's. It is possible to share the lessons and practices that I use to stay aware. By being aware, discomfort of any kind can be managed.

In the past few years, I have adopted practices that support my success in living with pain. It is fair to say I have implemented methods that have allowed my personality to change just as well.

A time for gratitude

Before I leave my bed in the morning, I will think of three things to be grateful for. Having spent much of my life as a pessimist, at first this was not easy. In fact, I used the same three things every day for a long time. I was thankful for my husband, children, and my bed.

Eventually, I came to realize how fortunate I was in simple ways. I have indoor plumbing. The water can be hot within a few seconds. Everything I need is conveniently located on the main floor of my house. Our animals give me unconditional love daily! Okay, that might be a stretch. They are cats, and if the food goes away, the love might, too, but I digress.

My roof doesn't leak. My imagination is still intense and vibrant. There are clothes in my closet, and I choose whatever I want to wear. One of my favorite things to be grateful for is my powerful left leg. Trust me, my left leg has gone unappreciated for far too long. If you could see the diminished scale of my right leg, you'd understand. I stand up every morning by the grace of my insanely powerful left leg! Not to mention, my fingers work, and I can still type.

The list of things to be grateful for is unending. It is strange and sad how often I would get out of bed with anything less than gratitude. Make time to be grateful for the things habitually overlooked. It makes a difference in your thought process.

If someone is continuously looking for the light, they aren't focusing on darkness.

Make the bed

I was quick to dismiss this tip as idiotic when I first heard it. I mean, what good is making a bed going to do for anyone? For the longest time, I only left my bed for an hour at a time. I wasn't going to waste my motions on the hassle of a few blankets. If my body needed to be in bed, I wasn't going to sweat the small stuff.

I have made my bed every day since I've become stronger. Why? Because I've come to understand its significance beyond visual appeal. Making my bed is the first action of body movement. Plus, it's entirely selfish.

That is not just my bed. That is my sanctuary for relaxation, relief, and sleep. With gratitude in mind, that bed held me through a lot of long days and nights.

I look forward to the end of my day, knowing that one piece of furniture cradles this body perfectly. Therefore, that bed is going to look comfortable and inviting.

Pulling up the blankets is a mindful moment. It's a gentle transition from sleep to adventure. I am going to keep my space clean and warm, ready for the next use. While doing this, I'm deliberately thinking about all of the muscles I am using and warming up for the day. I'm considering all the movements that I could not perform a few years ago.

Whenever I enter my room, that beautiful bed is ready for me. This is a symbol of my private space. It is where I go to heal. It is a clean and organized oasis dedicated to recovery and rest.

Allow yourself to have days in bed. Allow yourself to be lazy when you need it. Then, when life calls you to adventure further, make the bed for when you return to your place of peace.

Wear the sparkle

Often, during my new adventures, situations arise that I would typically want to escape. People converse over politics and religion, gossip or judgmental topics. There is no longer a desire to stay in negative conversation. Believe it or not, being situationally unsettled could change my focus straight to any physical discomfort. I'd use my pain to escape a phone call, if I could.

Prior to my change in consciousness, I would have offered my own negative opinions. Most of the time, this was done obnoxiously ...and with my own brand of crazy. If anyone disagreed with me, I'd start an argument without hesitation. Now, things are vastly different. I don't have to take anything more seriously than is required.

I wear a silver bracelet with a metal bead in the center. It is not new or impressive, but it does serve a fantastic purpose. It sparkles when the light hits it just right. I notice this bracelet quite often.

When I am facing a family gathering, my husband's work event, or a day out with my kids, I wear this sparkle. Whenever its reflection catches my eye, I take a deep breath and look around my surroundings. This brings me peace and presence in the moment.

Where am I? Who am I with? What can I determine with my five senses? These are the first things I consider when my bracelet sparkles. This is a moment to take in my surroundings.

Then, I pay attention to something other than my mind-chattering thoughts. What can I hear besides the conversation? Is the air I am breathing fresh? Does it have a scent? What does the surface I am sitting on feel like? Am I enjoying the conversation or is this something I can change?

That bracelet is my reminder that I am okay. I am fully experiencing the moment for all it is worth. After all, I worked hard to get here. The moment I see that sparkle, I am grateful!

In fact, I like to think of that moment of sparkle as if it is myself, in a way. I am the only observer of my experience. I'm aware this life is led by my choices! I am out of my bed and experiencing something new. After a year of wearing the same bracelet, I find myself looking for it without the random flash of light. My awareness craves that selfish moment of taking in the surroundings.

I believe this little visual aid has helped me become a better listener. I am aware of conversation more completely and I seem to have an easier time responding to people. That moment of awareness comforts me. I can look around me, notice my five senses, and remind myself how far I have come.

No matter what else is going on, that shimmer on my wrist is meant for me. I brought that to my day, and it serves an enormous purpose, keeping me present and aware. That little sparkle helps bring peace and clarity into every day.

Be ready for something, and anything is possible

Getting dressed in the morning isn't always on my list of priorities. Most of it is due to physical comfort. The rest is because I do not leave my house every day. Still, I have noticed that by getting dressed, I am more likely to seek out adventure and accept opportunities.

My best friend gave me a solid and brilliant piece of advice. Leave your shoes on!

I love that! If my shoes are on, I'm likely to get up more often. I'm likely to step outside to get the mail. It's even increased the probability of me going out to lunch or running my errands. What a great piece of advice! Leave your shoes on. It's simple, small, and best of all, it works for me!

I allow my body to rest when discomfort requires calm attention. Still, by being ready for anything to happen, I am more likely to say 'Yes' to new possibilities.

Saying, "Yes"!

Where has the answer, "No," ever taken you when given a new opportunity?

I was the queen of saying, "No!"

Putting myself in a public situation, especially with family or friends, was a nightmare. My default response was always a firm "No." Sometimes, if I really wanted to be nice to people, I would say, "I'll think about it." Even small or private affairs held so many dependencies that I usually refused to attend.

As my behaviors and attitude began to shift, I had an epiphany. Each time I refused an offer, I was losing the opportunity for anything extraordinary to unfold. I was blocking my own chance at growth. It's kind of like the universe was knocking at my door and I refused to open it.

Accepting an invitation is challenging, especially if it is new or preceded by a negative experience. Our minds play out negative scenarios long before we've given our answer to an invite. Some of us have programmed ourselves to see the worst possible outcome every time.

Recently, I've been embracing the power of "Yes" to situations that previously turned into nightmares. Sure, there's a chance that things could go wrong again. But if I don't grant myself the opportunity, I'll never witness what could go right.

I remember my son inviting me to a Renaissance fair the year I began adventuring out of the house. This was completely new to both of us! It required a long car ride, expensive food without any control over the ingredients, and walking ... lots of walking. My husband had no interest and had been working under pressure. So, it was up to me to decide if I was going to take all these unbelievable risks without his support. Nothing would stop me from saying, "yes" to my son.

I felt like I was going to die! The whole morning as we got ready, my heart was having a tribal drum ceremony. My hands were shaking. Everything that could perspire was leaking. But I was still dead set that I was going to do it.

It was one of my best memories of the last decade. My son and I had an absolute blast. Yes, I was uncomfortable with walking. I stopped every fifty feet to rest and take in my surroundings. The food was not good for me, and I ended up being hungry for most of the day. Still, I would not change a single moment! My son had a blast with all of the costumes, leatherwork, and blacksmithing. It was by far the best adventure we have had together as adults.

Since then, I have said "Yes" to the most terrifying things. Prior to my conscious experience, heights were terrifying. Would you believe I have driven up the Rocky Mountains and the Appalachian Mountains?

I'm not going to lie. The first time I got on a plane with my husband, I stopped when reaching the threshold of the passenger boarding bridge. In a single second, I became severely aware of my prior terror of heights. Surprisingly, instead of ideas of falling or crashing, my mind held one thought. It was simple and profound. I was willing to die to experience that adventure with my husband. After that moment, the fear was extinguished.

Still, I couldn't help but notice the same profound emotion that I felt when my son and I went to the Ren-Faire. It was then, it dawned on me. I can consciously manipulate fear.

It turns out that fear and excitement have the same chemical physiology in our bodies. I chose to take the fear of a moment and turn it into excitement.

Once I crossed that threshold and entered the plane, I was absolutely fine and interested in every detail of what I was experiencing. Guess what? I love flying! Taking off and touching down are just as exciting as a roller coaster.

I would never have learned how exciting life could be without the courage to say, "Yes"!

Use the crutch!

There is no need to "tough it out" when you're having a difficult time functioning with pain. No one else is suffering from your pain or illness. If I need to use medication, disability aids, handicapped parking, or anything else that brings me comfort, you can bet I am going to use it!

I choose what is suitable for me.

It wasn't just the wheelchair, plant medicine, and parking spaces I took advantage of. I have a handheld grabbing device that allows me to pick up items off of the floor, open my curtains without bending forward and reach whatever is needed. I use small AI devices in my home for security. If an injury occurs and I need to contact someone for help, that device gives me a sense of self-security. Also, the electric carts in the shopping centers ...I used those religiously before getting my own wheels.

The point is, if there is a device or medication that allows you freedom from discomfort, use it! You are the only one living in your body. Do whatever it takes to keep moving forward.

Plant medicine played a vital role in my early days of healing. This body was sick and near death... and I wanted to explore every available avenue to find comfort. As it turned out, that medication may have sped up my healing. It helped my pain in a way nothing had accomplished before. I could eat, digest food, and even sleep.

When it comes to my own life, I'm choosing to be selfish. I'm prioritizing my well-being and what I believe will give me the best chance of living a fulfilling life. It's a decision I've made with careful consideration and a focus on my own needs and health.

After a while, I became healthier and did not need medication as I had before. My body allowed digestion more, my pain was manageable with meditation and personal understanding, and I was beginning to heal.

I cannot say that strongly enough. If you are dealing with pain and suffering, don't hesitate to do whatever you need to do to keep going. Use the crutch!

There are people in my life that simply refuse to use any type of stability assistance. They believe that a cane, walker, or wheelchair is embarrassing. The concept of "use it or lose it" is always in their mind. I think this idea is useful and keeps people motivated.

When I suggest using the crutch, I'm talking about meeting opportunities when you are challenged by discomfort. At my worst, I stopped enjoying life. I didn't take my wheelchair to the zoo with my family. I didn't use my cane at social functions. It was easier to simply stay home. So, I stayed home for years.

When I started shifting into conscious moments. I recognized my need of assistance almost all of the time. My husband bought me a collapsable cane to keep in the car and I used it for everything. Here is the great part. When I say I used it for everything, I mean adventures! I was leaving the house for shopping trips, short walks outside and holiday events. Instead of staying home, I risked looking weak. This made me stronger! The physical exercise was great for my body, and the social interaction was great for my well-being. These little voyages let me experience life. I was experiencing adventure even though I still dealt with pain.

I won't wait any longer. My existence is happening now! I don't want to miss anything anymore. Therefore, I will use the crutch!

Let the pain come

I have learned to trust my body.

When pain comes, either in the form of stabbing in the lumbar region, aching legs, burning in the upper spinal column, or simple knee agony, I have learned how to adjust. I embrace pain completely.

For some aches and discomfort a simple anti-inflammatory will help. For bone pain, I rely on using ice or heat, depending on the sensation. These aids allow me to maintain mobility and a life of adventure. As for the pelvic pain and spine burning between my shoulder blades and neck ... that is a different story. It seems to defy consolation.

This is where I've honed my resilience. This is why I've embraced meditation.

I will sit in my most comfortable chair and selfishly claim this time for myself. Here, I allow my body and pain to exist without judgment or interference. It's a sanctuary of self-care amidst the chaos of discomfort. Yes, sitting still and silent can be frustrating but I refuse to let those emotions overpower me.

The battle is in consciously choosing *not* to feel emotions brought on by thought. I do this by reminding myself, it's never a good idea to let events compile into problems. A headache in the morning is not the same moment as a stomachache in the afternoon. There were hours of events between those issues. Acknowledging all of the good events is a powerful way to avoid problem compilation with emotional thought. Setting emotion aside, I'm able to focus on the immediate moment of pain.

Instead, I will settle my mind and thoughts into the intricate details of my pain.

I visualize the body beneath the muscle and inside the bones. My imagination tries to picture exactly what tendons, nerves, and ligaments look like at that moment. Does pain give the internal landscape a different color? A common cold will make your cheeks red and bumping your knee will cause it to swell up with fluid. Therefore, there might be some visible internal difference. When pain comes, I visualize what could be taking place deep within this body. Then, I consider the location of pain being supported by systems that have never received credit.

This takes patience and gentle kindness on my part. I visualize my muscles easing and imagine the tendons and ligaments softening, nurturing my body through this process. The crucial aspect of dealing with pain is to endure the moments without negative emotion. This moment is temporary. The intense feeling of pain will change.

My body knows what it is doing. It has spent years healing injuries, scratches, sprains, and aches. The synovial fluid within the joints is there to protect the area and cushion any impact. It has done this job throughout my existence without a single ounce of recognition. Cortisol works to decrease inflammation and strengthen immune response. This has always happened without mental thoughts dictating any action.

The body knows what to do! The body knows how to heal, adapt, and overcome injury.

I was simply too impatient to let my body heal in its own time. Not to mention, I was too stubborn and pompous to simply accept the pain. These days, I have learned to appreciate this fantastically intricate corporeal form. I've learned to let the pain come and allow my body to process healing in the best way it sees fit.

While I acknowledge moments of pain, deep breathing and visualization shift my focus away from feelings of desperation. Again, this is a selfish moment of meditation or mindfulness. Instead of missing moments of joy, disappointing others, or feeling sorry for myself, I find peace and clarity through these techniques. I rely on the trust I have for this body and sit in quiet peace.

When pain is with me, I know that my body is enacting countless intricate tasks unseen by the eye and overlooked by medical professionals. This has been my experience. This body will return to its natural state. In time, I will return to my level of normal activity. All I must do is give it the time and respect it requires.

Pain is an intricate part of my life. Still, I can thrive despite these moments. I will be patient. I will be good to myself. It is my choice to let the pain come.

Meditation as a medication

My journey with meditation is taking me further than I have ever dreamed.

For nearly a decade, meditation had been suggested to me. At least two dozen times throughout my medical and mental healthcare experience, some jerk would ask me if I meditated. Each time, I scoffed at the idea of such a notion.

I'd get angry that people thought my pain was, you know, "all in my head." How many times have I heard that? It infuriated me that those people assumed sitting with my eyes closed and focusing on my breath was going to fix my 'genuine' problems. So, if you're rolling your eyes right now, I understand.

As I became severely sick, I turned to "self-help" audio recordings and videos. My body was no longer capable of much activity and listening to music and stories became a solace.

However, as I was avoiding meditation, I noticed something different just at the edge of sleep. It took several nights to realize what was happening, but I began to acknowledge my pain under deep relaxation without having it bother me.

I really wish there were another way to describe that feeling. All of the alarms and whistles of pain were still there. However, my body relaxed, and my mind, without being asleep, let the alarms and whistles slip into the background of my consciousness. It was the closest I had been to feeling zero pain.

The sensations of illness and discomfort, though remaining, did not cause me to move or strain to fight against them. When seriously ill, I could enter that relaxed state and allow the digestive cramps to remain as they were without needing to engage them. I was meditating long before I understood what was happening.

I'm not going to suggest meditation fixes everything (although I believe, in a way, it does). What I will say is one can find a way to be more active and less traumatized by pain with meditation practice.

Meditation is a gateway to understanding consciousness and acknowledging the body and mind as distinct from the inner self.

Mindfulness / Meditation with others

Almost everything in this book has to do with mindfulness, the act of being aware without judgment. I think, if I had a way to describe an average day in my life, it would be simply mindful.

Mindfulness has become very popular in today's culture. It has had such an impact that schools are beginning to implement mindful moments throughout the day to encourage awareness and kindness to children. Social media has unending groups for conscious awareness. Even hospitals and nursing homes are implementing this routine into their daily activities.

Another one of my exciting adventures was going to a library and trying out a mindfulness class. I am grateful for my mindfulness group. My life needed new experiences with people who were hopeful, kind, and determined to live a better life. I wasn't sure where to start looking.

I've never minded being in big crowds. People watching was a hobby. With a love of writing, (never mind the level of talent) I would see characters and stories everywhere I went.

However, I didn't want to be a noticeable part of the crowd. This mindfulness group was bound to be small, and I was going to be noticed.

Initially, the idea of repeatedly leaving the house to sit quietly in a room with other people seemed bizarre. I had a ton of experience with doctors, but my experience with ordinary people had always been limited. Now, I found myself sitting with others, closing my eyes, and focusing on my breath for several minutes at a time. I was forming positive intentions and redirecting my thoughts on a regular basis.

This was not something I was comfortable with, at first. Yet, the class I walked into at my local library has added so much joy to my life.

Our instructor possessed an incredible ability to create a welcoming and comfortable atmosphere for everyone. She answered our questions and had an instinctive knack for knowing what we needed to focus on each session. We were all treated like individuals and found a profound sense of support within the group.

I found the community I was looking for, that day. There were even a few people, just like me, dealing with pain and suffering. We shared our experiences and challenges as equals and friends. It may be just a mindfulness group, but this became my therapy.

If you are looking to invest in yourself and meet new people, I suggest mindfulness and support group settings to everyone.

Hold the desire to create opinions

One of the most significant and recent changes is learning to hold my opinions. Much of this comes from awareness. Some of it comes from meditation practice. I've learned to be okay with things the way they are instead of trying to control outcomes. There is a deeper understanding of balance in my life.

It is easy to jump on a judgment. Just this week, a dozen short videos, news headlines, text messages, and phone conversations brought forth unconscious opinions. Well, they are unconscious for as long as I allowed them to be.

Opinions help us meet like-minded people. They help us decide where and when boundaries are needed. It may be fair to say opinions can keep us safe. I'm at a place in my life where I am reevaluating my opinions on an 'as needed' basis. Except now, I try not to let my opinions run without awareness.

I continually remind myself that my judgment isn't always necessary. My view of a situation or idea is not essential unless someone asks me for a different perspective.

To be completely honest, I rarely need to form an opinion in the first place. While initially frustrating and unnatural, I've come to understand that crafting opinions stems from my desire to sway things toward my will. This means, I'm not accepting people for who they are. I'm not accepting the situation as it is. I want to change it ...with my opinion.

Not only is forming opinions a strong desire, but it usually comes with a lot of emotion. If the subject and story do not agree with my personal experiences the emotion that ties with the judgment is negative.

This is where self-boundaries are extremely useful and keep me in a peaceful state. When confronted with a situation that brings up a judgment, I take a second to pause and assess the need for my attention. I'll talk about taking five deep breaths a little later. However, when opinions arise it is a good time to check in with one's thoughts.

This allows a distinct gap of time between visual or verbal stimulus and reaction. In that space of awareness, I look at the way my thoughts form and decide if they are necessary or simply entertaining. I don't want to waste any more time creating emotion for the sake of having an emotion.

I have no desire to be negative. It is within my power to choose a better emotion. To do this, I try to hold the desire to create opinions.

Raise the bar on self-talk

We can really get stuck in our thoughts and self-talk. Our ego builds itself upon a platform of given information, trauma, experience, and personal views.

The phrase, "I can't," was likely the most common thing I would tell myself.

I convinced myself I was incapable, ugly, lazy and unlovable ...destined for abandonment. Being a recovering alcoholic and drug user, I believed I had no self-control and made ridiculous decisions. I doubted my talents and purpose.

My children loved their father more. I didn't finish college and would never be intelligent. I was hyper, obnoxious, lazy, and self-centered. I told myself these lies. Worse yet, I believed them.

When we are fighting illness and pain, our thoughts can be worse than the pain. The simple dislike of ourselves becomes a complicated domino effect that can even cause our bodies to rage against us.

Thinking negatively about our personal traits is far too easy!

Even though we have let it become an automatic response in our minds, they are still just mind-made thoughts. Hardly anything we think is a fact. It is simply a distorted point of view.

I did not come into my new awareness without the rude self-talk. Yes, I did have a space between judging myself and reacting to the judgment. Still, the tendency to think of myself poorly is still there, right behind my consciousness. I'm just not entertaining it these days.

I've taken some time to face the person in the mirror. I remind my reflection that I am no longer my own enemy. Whenever possible, I compliment myself. If a mistake happens and I instinctively berate myself, I say three positive things as quickly as possible to make up for the misstep. Not only that, but I use that reflection to deal with my pain and illness. When having a rough moment (keeping in mind it is only that moment and will change) I share my pride with that reflection. I thank that woman looking back at me for her strength and compassion.

Yes, this may sound ridiculous. In my opinion, it is no more foolish than hating the only body I have or despising the only person I could ever be.

Love yourself relentlessly. We give strangers more compassion than we give ourselves. When will we learn that we are worthy of our own empathy and respect?

Laugh at every chance

Laughter is incredibly beneficial for your mind and your body! It is great for your heart, boosts your immune system, and helps reduce stress levels. Laughter is so good for you; it doesn't matter if you fake it until you make it. Your body reacts to it as if it's the real deal. So go ahead, laugh as much as you can. It's one of the best things you can do for your overall health and well-being!

Have you ever been laughing so hard it hurts? Or is it hurting so much that more laughter causes you to have to change physical position? Guess what? It's still good for you! Even in those moments of discomfort, laughter continues to work its wonders on your mind and body.

I have an enthusiastic sense of humor. On those occasions, I bow to the artistry of the internet! I have a few choice websites I love to visit when in need of a good chuckle. When that fails, I'll bring on standup comedy, jokes, and memes. Everything is available to us in the internet age. This is seriously beneficial when going out with friends needs to be postponed.

Keep on laughing!

Learn something new ... as often as you can

As an observer of this life and my time on this planet, I've come to understand the beauty of knowledge.

As children, we are placed in learning centers and given a strict diet of social expectations and forced historical views presented as fact. In the late 60's, NASA conducted a study of creative genius in children and found that over 95% of young children under age six were creative geniuses. This percentage decreased significantly by the time children were in their teenage years, to less than 20%. The number of creative genius people plummeted to less than 5% in adulthood. This study expressed the belief that the change was due to typical education. Land, George. NASA Creativity Study. NASA, 1968.

This information is relevant to me for one reason. It reminds me that I have choices that were not available when I attended school. We are no longer restricted by subjects or timeframes. We can learn about anything at any time. This is an incredible freedom! Let's recover our percentage of genius.

We live in a world connected by invisible threads of increasing information. There is data about the past, the present, and the probable future. It's always available to me. I can get up at two o'clock in the morning and investigate Egypt's great pyramid using a dozen different resources without leaving my bed. Plus, there are no restrictions or rules about how or what I want to learn.

I'm going to take advantage of this opportunity! My favorite area of study at the moment is neuroplasticity. Incredible breakthroughs in brain function and information pathways are currently being discovered. I have no doubt remarkable things will stem from the advancement of this study. Perhaps we will learn new ways to improve our understanding of pain and how to decrease the impact it has on our lives.

To put it simply, learning keeps me mentally younger, youthfully curious, connected, and conversational. It creates new thoughts and leaves less room for negative habits.

Forgive myself

None of the events in my life made sense. There was a time my journals and memories were filled with drama and turmoil. It was one negative event after another. That is, until I became aware of the part I played in the creation of my history. None of it should have happened the way it did. Then again, it could never have gone any differently ...because it didn't. Only perception can change the past.

I've taken people and opportunities for granted. There is every reason to hold myself at fault for the events that brought pain and illness. However, there is one constant fact to keep in mind. The past does not matter, right now. Not to mention, I'm kind of tired of living there.

At the time of every poor choice, every unwise decision, and each defining moment, I did not hold different or better information. There was no way of avoiding a future I could not predict.

When my consciousness allowed me to see my life as it is, not as I imagined, I realized many mistakes. My husband suffered, my children suffered, and many people were affected by my choices. Damn, I not only hurt those around me, but I also did quite a lot of damage to this body.

I asked for those treatments. I agreed to my doctors' suggestions. I insisted on a second spinal cord stimulator. Still, none of it matters at this moment!

The person I was, at that time, did the best I could with what I knew. Those choices were difficult. Now, the damage is being healed with conscious presence. I'm not working my butt off to make amends. I've apologized to my children. I've apologized to my husband. However, I have no desire to despise the warrior I had to be at that time.

That woman, stuck in bed and giving up, had to endure those moments in order to tell this story. Every decision made has led me to this point.

Therefore, I forgive myself!

I forgive myself for not behaving better. I forgive myself for not being stronger. I forgive myself for all my faults! I forgive myself for not loving myself better when I needed it the most.

Today is a new opportunity. I cannot move freely into the future if I'm desperately regretting the drama of my past.

The harmful effect of complaining and pain compilation

When my back and legs hurt, I let everyone know. When I couldn't move my neck, had a swollen knee, or pain from injections and nerve burns, I told the world how it felt. What I didn't understand was how complaining created more suffering.

It became routine to complain about pain. I never stopped to think about how much credit I was giving to the dysfunctions and taking away from my success.

When I complained about the way I felt, it was never just about that particular moment. No, my pain had become massive. It had its own gravity, sucking in momentous events, fun, achievements, and desires. The pain that began as a few difficult moments grew into something completely unmanageable.

During the intense moments of pain, I wasn't just complaining about that particular moment. It was all of the moments. The failure of every medication. The frustration about each piece of life that had been taken away. I was angry over events I was missing and people I couldn't see. Then, when the next intense painful swing would occur, all those complaints would add up into one addicting thought process. I now refer to this thought process as pain compilation.

Pain compilation was how my thought process stole my life. I was so busy focusing on the complaints that I ignored the joy. It took a couple of years to understand that this had become a part of my personality. However, now that I know this is a behavior, it's easier to recognize and slow down. We all go through serious down days with pain. The trick is to avoid pain compilation. I try not to let a couple bad days ruin a whole week.

Complaining served a purpose when talking with my pain management team and discussing treatment plans with my doctors.

Let me say again: complaining served a purpose when it was shared with my care team.

Now, let me explain how complaining had an adverse effect on my beliefs.

"I'm at my limit! I can't take it anymore!"

Those sentences ignore one fact: I could, and I did.

Gratitude is enormously powerful, but it takes practice and patience, especially after decades of grumbling about everything. When I complained, there was no room for gratitude.

The only thing left in my focus was how horribly my dysfunctions affected me.

I fight to find reasons for gratitude. There are still moments when I double over and stop breathing due to physical discomfort. However, now I acknowledge that I am a champion.

This feeling is not the worst I have endured. It is what I am experiencing at that current moment, and it will not last for long. I'm not going to let it compile into something more dramatic.

It took patience and practice. I learned to separate the moments of pain from the years of dysfunction. This was done by complaining less and reminding myself of how strong I had become. There is a time when complaining is necessary. Likewise, there is a time to celebrate the small wins that bring stronger days and better adventures.

Take five deep breaths

This advice is a gem! I use it several times a day. I often overstate it to my friends and family. Just take five deep breaths!

You'd be surprised how quickly the ability to stop and recenter yourself can change your emotions and assist with physical pain. It is not just breathing deeply while your mind waddles over your current situation, either. When I suggest taking five deep breaths, I mean using that opportunity. This is time to consider unconscious thought or opinions. Am I speaking or thinking harshly toward myself or others? How does my body feel at this moment. Am I capable of making any discomfort better? What is the best way to improve both my mind and my body right now?

Conscious breathing entails experiencing the air as it moves through the body. Notice the temperature change that takes place in your lungs. Whatever is going on around you can fade into the background. There is now space between you and any situation. The breath allows your body to communicate if pain is present.

In these quiet moments, your body will tell you what it needs. Perhaps you need to lie down, slow down, or move your body more. Your awareness changes from mind-made thoughts to the acknowledgment of how best to serve yourself. Use the timespan of five deep breaths to bring your focus back where it is needed ...back to yourself.

This is your life. This is your body. What do you need to do or not do at this moment? Use that extended time entirely selfishly. Be at peace while you take five deep breaths. This is a peaceful and easy act of taking care of yourself.

"Pain is inevitable suffering is optional" - Haruki Murakami

If it's out of my hands, keep it out of my head

This realization came to me the first day of my conscious awareness. The world is full of drama. Global events can be overwhelming and seem catastrophic. Local issues and family affairs can lead one to wonder, what am I going to do? Well, sometimes the only thing I have to do is take five deep breaths. If I cannot change the situation or have any effect on the outcome of a circumstance, it is best to just ...let it go.

Let the whole thought, idea, and problem leave your mind. We are geared toward drama and theory. We know that television and news sell better if the headlines are negative and fear-provoking. However, we do not have to suffer holding these thoughts and letting them run amuck in our minds.

It is difficult to recognize when your thoughts are running a race they cannot win. If you are lucky enough to catch yourself having this issue, there is a way to stop it. Consider the main problem that is worrying you and then ask yourself one question. "Can I do anything about it?"

If you can, then it is time to take action to improve the situation. If you cannot do anything about it, shake it off. Literally, shake your hands, move your body, and step away from the area you are in at that moment. Make the moment physical instead of emotional. The recognition of mental spiraling is difficult, but essential.

Once your mind is free, you can consider the positive changes you can make. You can find better uses for your imagination. With gratitude, hopelessness tends to fade into the background.

As I've said before, there are people all over the world twenty-four hours a day in need of communication. It may not be possible to make an impact on the entire world, but you can help one person by giving them your attention. Doing one good thing can change your focus and help someone else with theirs.

Let go of what you cannot control and offer your hand to help in any way you are able.

Mental Conditioning

(This is not for everyone)

"I like it."

What do I like? The uncontrollable discomfort that comes out of nowhere. Yup, "I like it".

This was my mantra for many weeks.

The crazy jolt of electrical pain in my spine that can't be stopped and won't quit. "I like it". The challenge that comes when you have to perform life skills like sitting down, standing up, or lying in bed. "I like it". Feeling nauseous and often unable to support digestion. "I like it". All of it!

This is what I tell myself. This is what I say to the reflection in the mirror.

The intense joint-solidifying cold of a Wisconsin winter in a stone house with a million and one drafts. "I like it".

When I'm tired and forced to function while enduring physical sensations that used to stop me in my tracks. I state out loud, "I like it".

Perhaps you've seen movies depicting military personnel enduring rigorous training in harsh weather conditions. Rain pelts down on them as they hold their rifles above their heads, marching in step while repeating cadences in freezing temperatures. A stern Drill Sergeant stands before them, demanding, "You like it!" And in response, the soldiers are compelled to echo back, "I like it!" This was done to manipulate their minds into controlling their body.

Well, I figured I would try it. Let me remind you that I am not a professional in anything other than my life. I was willing to try anything to retrain my brain into overcoming my disabilities.

Guess what? I found it helped.

At first, this was said in hatred of the present pain or suffering. "I like it!" With my teeth ground, jaw clenched, fists at my sides, the words burned my throat.

After a while, it was said in anger and frustration with a hint of patronization. "I like it...."

Then, there was utterly crazy rage. "I like it!"

After a few weeks, it became simply annoying. "I like it. I like it. I like it."

No, change didn't happen overnight. Yes, friends and family thought I had lost any remaining common sense. At no point was I going to disagree with them. I had cracked – but not in the wrong way.

After a couple of months, something strange happened. I didn't mind the discomfort so much. The phrase became my shield. I could find stability in the words, and the discomfort did not control me the same way it once had.

I could work through the pain. I could walk through the discomfort. I could eat through the illness. I could manage whatever this body went through because... well ... I liked it.

It makes sense to me at this phase in life. I can teach myself to endure what would be labeled a "bad moment" by believing that I like whatever moment I am having.

My mind is being trained to tolerate sickness and discomfort. Three words are my shield. Three words are my armor. Three words get me through the roughest times.

And ..."I like it."

Sound therapy is beneficial

Music has always been therapeutic. It is the simplest form of magic. Music helps create emotion in films and theater work. It empowers us to tackle the challenges of our day, persevere through demanding exercise routines, and soothes us into peaceful sleep at night.

Most of us can think of at least one particular song that causes us to drive a little over the speed limit. It raises our heartbeat and puts a smile on our face.

This is true, with sound being beneficial to pain as well. There has been immense study into sound vibration and how it can promote healing.

I'm not going to delve deep into this topic. What works for me is not always going to work for anyone else. My body has learned to tolerate intense moments of pain better with sound therapy.

I meditate better with soft music. I use ambient sounds during my day. Drum solos and Tibetan bowls help me tolerate painful flare-ups. Then, at night, the crickets and thunderstorms surround me before I sleep. Sound has been instrumental in my self-healing journey.

That's it!

Those are the more prominent tips and tricks I use to live a more conscious and adventurous life with physical pain.

This was not a 'to-do' list. These happened to be the tools I used to find my path. Perhaps one or two ideas will work for someone else.

I hope everyone dealing with pain finds the tools they need to function just a little bit better. Keep searching for whatever is suitable for you!

Chapter Six
Facts and Opinions

Pain changes inside the brain over time.

The battle with pain is not being ignored in the medical field. Doctors and scientists are using brain scans and imaging techniques to learn how the brain processes pain. Numerous studies have been undertaken, and ongoing research continues.

The following research has created intense new curiosities in my awareness.

Hashmi, J. A. et al. (2013). *Shape shifting pain: Chronification of back pain shifts brain representation from nociceptive to emotional circuits. Brain, 136(9), 2751–2768.*

This study pertains to the result of brain scans for patients experiencing back pain after injury. One hundred and twenty patients received brain scans four times a year for one year. However, not every participant remained in the study for various reasons.

These scans began within weeks after the initial injury to get a baseline view of what pain looks like inside the brain. Then, the study follows the change in the patient's brain with new scans a year after the onset of pain.

Within this study, brain scans reveal heightened activity in regions such as the Anterior Cingulate Cortex, Thalamus, and Insula. These regions are recognized as conventional pain-processing areas within the brain. In other words, this is the location a doctor would expect to find changes after initial injury.

Not everyone in the study developed chronic pain. Some healed completely and had little loss of function within months after their injury. Others developed long-term chronic pain.

What I found fascinating were the brain scans for the patients who developed chronic pain. These scans changed drastically within a year after injury.

The areas of the brain that originally detected the influx of pain no longer showed the same result. In fact, repeat scans showed that pain detection had been shifted to other locations of the brain. Instead of pain reception lingering in the typical pain-processing areas, these signals had migrated to the Medial Prefrontal Cortex. This is primarily the area of the brain associated with ...learning and emotion. It also assists with memory retrieval.

Does this mean that our bodies are learning pain? Is the brain moving short term information into long term memory? Does our emotional response to pain affect how our brains process sensations? Perhaps our bodies have felt a particular way for so long that the brain is simply forced to adjust. This makes sense from my perspective.

I would have loved to have taken part in a study like this. I've experienced different types of pain several times in my life. I know pain in a way that someone else knows a hobby or skill.

However, while my body deteriorated, it did not experience further procedural damage. I stopped the radio frequency ablations (nerve burns). I refused further surgeries. The procedures that created pain were stopped. Yet, I still feel random discomfort years after. Have I learned how to feel this way?

This is still painful! No matter where the brain shows it or how the doctors look at it, the pain persists. It is still genuine!

However, I must question my personal abilities. If my brain can learn to change where it processes pain, as shown within the forementioned study, can I ...unlearn pain? For this, I do not have an answer, but I am investigating the possibilities. Keep in mind, this is not meant for new traumatic injuries or when I clumsily whack my knee into a table. I am strictly speaking of chronic pain signals.

Opioids vs Antidepressants

Personal emotions run a little high with this subject, and I have considered my thoughts carefully. It is not an intention to promote any form of medication. However, as I have said before, use the crutch! Whatever you need to get by – USE IT!

It seems like everywhere doctors are taking patients off opioid medication such as hydrocodone and oxycodone. The uptick in trending treatment has been antidepressants. My personal experience with these medications has produced a significant opinion about the use of antidepressants for pain management.

I know, I know… I've already mentioned holding the desire to create opinions. Therefore, I will be speaking about my personal experience and what I learned from years of prescription management.

Treating pain with anti-depressants was both necessary and dangerous for me. This treatment was given under the claim that these complicated and long-lasting antidepressants are safer than opioid pain medicines.

An opioid medication will relieve pain. Opioids are a fast treatment and produce relief in a matter of minutes. If you break your leg and are given an opioid pain medication, most patients will feel significantly better very quickly.

An antidepressant is commonly used to treat mood disorders. These medications are not prescribed in the event of an injury. If you break your arm, the doctor will not give you an antidepressant. It takes weeks to months to feel the effect of an antidepressant. It will do no good for any immediate pain.

Antidepressants are widely prescribed for chronic pain. Perhaps the reason for the effectiveness is due to the studies of how the brain reacts to long-term pain. Perhaps their efficacy is due to a person's emotional trauma increasing pain sensations. However, in my opinion, the risks of depression medication may be far more dangerous than the risk of opioid medication.

According to the National Institute on Drug Abuse (NIDA) in 2014, prescription opioid pain medication is less addictive than alcohol or nicotine. Heroin is the most addictive opioid, and it is never used as a medication in the United States.

In the list of common side effects of opioids, you will find constipation, drowsiness, weakness, and indigestion. As uncomfortable as these side-effects seem, they are less severe than the side-effects of antidepressants. The side-effects for antidepressants include anxiety, weight gain, gastrointestinal issues, and an increase of suicidal thoughts. When someone is dealing with pain, disease, handicap and depression a medication that could possibly increase suicidal ideation is, in my opinion, a concerning thought.

After years of both opioid and antidepressant medications, my body has taught me to respect the adverse reactions and the effects of withdrawal.

While I was treated with opioids for pain, my doctor prescribed antidepressants long before I felt depressed. These medications were tacked on to my chart with the intention of relieving my pain. However, as years went on and my physical challenges waxed and waned, the need to use antidepressants became vital to my wellbeing.

As my journey of conscious healing began, I knew I wanted a release from prescription medications. I was no longer interested in putting anyone else in charge of my body. This was my newest goal. I had already acclimated to life after opioid dependency and felt ready for another challenge.

In hindsight, the withdrawal of opioids was far less serious and dangerous than the withdrawal of anti-depressants. This is strictly my opinion based on experience with both classes of medications.

When my body was going through opioid withdrawal, I experienced anxiety, nausea, upset stomach, and insomnia. This was difficult and uncomfortable. It took about two weeks to feel better and over a month to feel secure.

However, the withdrawal from antidepressants was seriously uncomfortable and lasted anywhere from six months to a year ...for each medication. I suffered confusion for weeks with intense headaches, dizziness, insomnia and mood swings. Those were just the easy symptoms.

Withdrawal from antidepressants was terrifying and it took months for the effects to subside. I felt electric shocks throughout my body and in my head. This lasted longer than my malfunctioning spinal cord stimulator. It was less intense but no less disturbing. My face and hands began to twitch. I felt muscle spasms almost everywhere. Somehow, each spasm brought on an influx of my familiar chronic pain. I was sensitive to light and noise and had a desire to cry or panic daily. This process was exhausting, even in my conscious state.

There is a condition called Antidepressant Discontinuation Syndrome (ADS). According to the Cleveland Clinic study from 2005 to 2007, 27% to 86% of patients who stop antidepressants, with or without healthcare supervision, experience some degree of ADS. This is concerning to me because the main complications of ADS are: mania, suicidal ideation, and suicide.

Use the crutch! Antidepressants are necessary for some patients and extremely useful! They have a respectable place in medical science. However, I believe opioid pain medication is more effective for pain and has less detrimental withdrawal symptoms.

Finally, here is where hope is hidden for those who suffer from chronic pain.

It's not just me!

People all over the world are awakening into presence and many of them are experiencing this process through incredible pain. This means that pain can change who you are in a good way!

For those with severe injury, unbearable illness, and longstanding discomfort, wouldn't it be great to believe that positive change can still happen? Can you imagine a life of activity, adventure, and hope? The fear of deterioration is natural with chronic pain. Let's set that fear aside for a moment.

I'm talking about real hope. Change can happen to anyone. Life can still be satisfying while experiencing singular moments of discomfort.

I am not in a different body. None of my dysfunctions or diseases have moved out! However, I am not the same person I was a few years ago. I am vibrant, gentle-working, happy and secure after being housebound and bedridden. Sure, I've gone through medical procedures and drug treatments that may have some screaming – "Oh, that is what healed her problem!"

Well, none of my diagnoses have changed. I am still handicapped with limitations. I simply do not suffer in my situation any longer.

It was awakening into conscious awareness that propelled me out of pain and back into life.

When this miracle happened to me, I dug into every podcast I could find about healing oneself. The endless videos on mindfulness, gratitude, and self-love propelled me into wanting better experiences than what pain had been supplying.

If you want to heal, if you want to increase happiness in your life, you're going to have to fight for it. It isn't really that hard, but it is time-consuming and takes relentless diligence. Fortunately, for many living with chronic pain, you are bound to have extra time on your hands.

Let me warn you. There are some awkward and interesting views out in the world on self-healing and conscious awareness. No doubt, I've researched at least twenty oddball videos or blogs for every piece of information that was relatable to my situation. That being said, you never know where you will find the chord that strikes with you.

Pain is a very personal experience, and there is no one right way to move forward. So, look at every path! Take a chance on anything that speaks to you.

Some people find healing with the power of faith. Some people dive head-first into spirituality and alternative medicine. You may scroll through the internet for days or hide in a library for a week before finding a direction of healing that speaks individually to you.

The best part is, once you have an interest in something ... anything that gives you hope, you've found something new to try. This new path might not include surgeries, procedures, or tests. It is simply information that empowers you.

Imagine getting up in the morning and doing things you couldn't do a year ago because you were too limited at that time. Suffering, in my opinion, really is a choice. What many of us forget is that healing and growth are a choice as well.

Remember, your body knows what to do. It has been trying to protect your wounds for as long as you have had them.

I really want to say, thank you for surviving your pain and taking steps to improve your life. You deserve recognition for the moments you have endured and I hope they become less severe and less often.

My experience of conscious awakening through pain has been extraordinary. I've acquired knowledge that has changed every fiber of my being. I've met people who have poured inspiration into me. The changes I've experienced in the past few years have been worth sharing.

I know great things are yet to happen. Sure, bad moments will come. Yes, there will be intense challenges. However, I will survive the trials ahead, knowing how much I have already accomplished. The aspect of pain will not rule this body. This is my life. I am going to live it with kindness, love and hope.

There is always hope.

You've come this far in your own story. There is no limit to how far you can go in your life. Thank you for listening to my experience. I wish you the best of luck on your own journey. Perhaps together we will evolve past chronic pain.

For other books by this author please
visit:

Ladybooks.life

www.ingramcontent.com/pod-product-compliance
Lightning Source LLC
Chambersburg PA
CBHW052009090426
42741CB00008B/1615